AN INHERITANCE

Based on true events

by

Brian Verity

2018

Copyright © Brian Verity

ISBN 978-1-911311-39-3

Printed by

Leiston Press,

Unit 1 - 1B Masterlord Ind Est,

Leiston, Suffolk IP16 4JD

Tel: 01728 833003

www.leistonpress.com

'Experience and reason have no necessary connection with one another'.

\-   Sir Kenneth Clark

'Oh good Horatio, what a wounded name,
Things standing thus unknown, shall live behind me!
If thou didst ever hold me in thy heart,
Absent thee from felicity a while,
And in this harsh world draw thy breath in pain,
To tell my story'.

\-   Hamlet, by William Shakespeare

CONTENTS

AN INHERITANCE

Chapter 1

"I SWEAR TO TELL THE TRUTH, THE WHOLE TRUTH, AND NOTHING BUT THE TRUTH". I repeat the well-known words in the cool and spacious committee room in the Civic Centre that is used as a Coroner's court. I am the first witness, I have little idea what will happen. I can remember only one previous occasion when I had been a witness in a court, and that was thirty-four years ago. There are few people present; the Coroner, seated alone amidst files on one side, a reporter opposite him, the Coroner's clerk and the pathologist at the top, the witnesses across the bottom. Hickman, the hospital registrar, looks hard at me. Even now, I have a slight feeling of triumph facing his concentrated, baleful stare. Whatever happens, Mary is dead. It is irrevocable, she is beyond them, the pity of it, but she is beyond them. I can rest a little on that, before the questioning begins.

* * *

I met Mary on my birthday, in 1959, at the Hammersmith Palais. The venue was banal, but at different times in the following years I facetiously remarked to friends, that Mary had been the best birthday present that I had ever received. In the previous eighteen months I had been through one of the worst periods of my life, with the breakdown of my first marriage, and a lengthy period of unemployment. The stress and consequent instability that it brought led to my admission as a voluntary patient to a mental hospital, where I had been prevailed upon to go for treatment. Within hours of my arrival I realised that I was saner than the staff and I had started moves to secure my discharge.

That had been in Norwich, and a few months later I moved to London, where I coped better with life, but it was meeting Mary that really transformed me from anxious suffering to relative peace and stability.

1

Her background was very different from mine. She was from Morayshire, and in her early years, during the 'thirties and 'forties, as the daughter of a farm labourer she had experienced unremitting poverty, with its consequent humiliations. Food was frequently bought on credit, and her parents would use her to face tradesmen to obtain more. She would usually possess just one dress and one pair of shoes, and would be under the threat of being put into tackety boots should she 'kick out' her shoes in the play of childhood. She was never put into these hob nailed boots that many of the boys wore. Some of the girls were made to wear them, and their example was a constant and frightening reminder of the humiliation that she might suffer. I believe that she would have gone barefoot first.

The poverty of her family ensured that she and her brother were made, like the other children, to do unpaid work about the farm by their father. She told me of the times when she had to spend long tiring hours lifting potatoes, or collecting sprouts in frosty weather, her fingers burning and aching with the cold, and she crying with pain.

She had also experienced the evils of the tied cottage system. Her father, less inclined than most to be servile with employers, was frequently fired and, each time the family home was lost along with the job. There was constant disruption of her schooling and her friendships with other girls. Some employers would show no respect to their employees, or their employees' families, and Mary told me about one laird who would unhesitatingly walk straight into their house, without first knocking, whenever he wanted to speak to Mary's father.

There was, too, the constant distress to the young Mary caused by the daily maltreatment of the farm animals; the big inoffensive Clydesdale horses that were worked unmercifully, the puppies about the farm to which she would be attached, which her father might arbitrarily destroy, swinging them by their hind legs so as to smash their heads against a wall, with the remark, "Too many bloody dogs about the place".

She had told me of the spaniel puppy that a boy-friend had given her, when she was a teenager. It was missing when she returned home one day. Her father had sold it while she was out, without her permission, and without any warning, and then pocketed the money. She never saw the pup again.

Sex was a source of embarrassment and shame to the adolescent Mary. She was then living in a narrow puritanical community, where any mention of it would draw sniggers from the young men, or stern disapproval from her elders. Sex, the greatest of pleasures, inevitably drew the greatest disapprobation from that pleasure-hating and work-oriented community. It was not until she came to the more liberal ambience of London and, in particular, was influenced by me, that she was able to separate sex from dirt. It was like so many of the changes that take place in our appraisal of life, often requiring only a conversation, or a passage from a book, to bring us naturally and smoothly to a deeper awareness of it.

Mary was small and sturdily built, with blue eyes, brown hair and regular features. She was conventionally pretty with a dazzlingly beautiful smile. She had exceptional physical stamina, and could easily outdistance me when we cycled together.

At the age of five she had put a lighted match to a twelve-bore cartridge carelessly discarded by her father. The resulting explosion had blown off the end digit of her left thumb, two digits of her index finger, and the end digit of her middle finger. This disfigurement was always fastened on by other children, who frequently taunted her. As an adult she habitually concealed the missing phalanges by keeping her fist clenched, and she would stuff cotton wool into the empty fingers of her gloves. She never played cards, or undertook any game or activity likely to reveal her left hand. Three months passed following our meeting at the Palais, and we had been several weeks in an intimate relationship, before I noticed that hand.

She was also conscious of her legs, which were slightly bowed because of malnutrition as a child. This had once been the cause of a bitter family row, when, as an adolescent, she first became aware of it as a disfigurement, and she had accused her father of neglect.

Her background, then, had been harsh, and her personal recollections of childhood were moving. She enriched my knowledge of rural poverty, which had previously been limited to the books on social history that I had read.

In spite of this she was sensitive and sympathetic. To cope with the tensions produced by this contradiction, and to defend herself against the rich pains of her emotions, she had come to face life with rigid inhibitions, when the need to shield her vulnerability arose. She was very dignified, and had fine judgement in knowing when to be silent and aloof in those situations where qualifying statements were unlikely to be understood. She was quite unsentimental herself and she usually recognised the spurious emotions and untrustworthy nature of people who were.

Because of her social background she had no vocational qualifications, and with her mutilated hand she was unable to take up that common standby, typing. She went straight from school on to the dole. Work was difficult to find for the unqualified in the immediate post-war years in that part of Scotland. She did find a job, eventually, as a cashier in a grocery store. Later she moved to Ballater, to work in a confectionery shop. This was a happy period for her. She had escaped from the sordid family background and the Moray Firth area, with its unpleasant associations. The shop owners provided her with her own room, and treated her kindly.

But it did not last. Under pressure from her brother and an aunt, Mary was persuaded to return to the family home, to act as housekeeper to her father. Rural social arrangements in Scotland at that time continued to require the sacrifice of daughters, rather than sons, to parental selfishness.

4

She did not remain at home for very long, and made what was to be the final break when she entered into nursing. She undertook a basic three years' training course at Aberdeen. Although she had the privacy of her own room in the nurses' residential block, she was hedged with restrictions, some of them arbitrarily imposed by the spinsterish females in the nursing chain of command. Pay, too, was very low. She obtained her nursing certificate, and moved to Glasgow with a Shetland friend, where they both trained as midwives.

Meanwhile, her brother had moved to London. Taking his advice she followed him in 1958 with all her 'estate', consisting of one suitcase and a paltry sum of money. He was instrumental in helping her to find work as a district nurse, and for the first months she lived with him and his wife, and their three young children. She then moved away into a bedsitting room, shortly before we met.

* * *

Soon after meeting Mary, she told me that her mother had died the previous year in Scotland, at the age of 53. Her death had come after many years of deterioration with a disease that had been called 'creeping paralysis', and her final five years were spent in hospital.

Mary had hated her mother. She recalled her mother's irrationality and paranoia, which had occurred daily. She gave, as an example, the day when she and her brother, as teenagers, had been romping about in a hay stack, and their mother had accused them of some undefined incestuous misdemeanour. She remembered that her mother was constantly dropping things, and in the years preceding her committal to hospital, she had needed walking sticks in order to move about.

Her father, during the years of her mother's deterioration, had been engaged in a number of extra-marital affairs. Widows seem to have been his forte, and it is likely that these unfortunate ladies would turn anywhere

5

for companionship and sexual contact, no matter how fleeting, to alleviate their own loneliness and deprivation. For him, these affairs would be a necessary escape from the stresses brought on by his wife's condition.

The hindsight that my experiences during recent years has given me confirm, that in addition to the poverty and cultural narrowness of the society into which she was born, Mary was under the pressure of a mother who was steadily declining physically and mentally, and a father, who, being denied the normal comforts of marital life, fled from the family home whenever he could, to gain solace wherever he could. Mary remembered the incessant tension and daily rows occasioned by this dreadful scenario; her father hard and conscienceless, her mother's pathological paranoia indistinguishable from the legitimate pain caused by her husband's philandering.

*   *   *

When Mary first talked to me about her mother and her childhood, in the early months of our relationship, I immediately remembered with surprise, that the childhood of my first wife had similarly been difficult. Her mother also suffered for many years from a progressive illness, affecting both her mind and her body. Although but middle-aged, she had spent her final years in a geriatric hospital, before dying. This disease, too, had been known as 'creeping paralysis'. No such vernacular name can be found in a medical dictionary, but at that time I was ignorant of this, and because of the symptomatic similarities between both mothers, I accepted that, unlikely though the name might be, both had probably died of the same disease.

Janice's background was very different from that of Mary. Her father was a property owner, mostly houses, and ran his own small boat-building yard on the east coast. She had not experienced material deprivation, but throughout childhood and adolescence she had, like Mary, suffered because of her mother's dementia and paranoiac behaviour. Janice clearly remembered her mother's suspicious personality and uncontrollable temper, and that she needed to use walking-sticks. Janice graphically described to me the chorea that her mother exhibited, and her mother's rolling eyes. With horror Janice remembered, that in the geriatric hospital in the final stages, her mother had been incontinent, and confined to a cot.

Janice's father had immersed himself in his business throughout the years of his wife's deterioration, and this had resulted in Janice bearing much of the responsibility for running the family home. As her mother steadily declined, Janice maturing, had been obliged to take charge of domestic matters. I had spoken to family friends, who told me what a terrible life Janice and her father had endured over many years.

An additional stress for Janice had been her fear that she might inherit this disease from her mother. Janice never mentioned that she had any specific reason for suspecting that it was hereditary, but it is possible, although speculative, that she may in childhood have overheard some chance remark from an adult, touching upon the existence of an hereditary disease in her mother's family. But her fears, though very real, were unfounded. When she was conscripted during the war, she learned that, in fact, she had been adopted by her parents as a young baby. She was not biologically related to her mother.

Again it is speculative, but did Janice's parents adopt her back in 1924, because they knew that there was a serious hereditary disorder in her mother's family, precluding them from having their own children? I will never know.

It was an unexpected shock for Janice to learn of her adoption at the age of 18. It explained a number of oddities about her childhood, notably that other children had pejoratively called her 'the orphan'. It appeared that everyone in that small, east coast town, had known that she had been adopted, except herself. Just as Mary's mutilated hand had drawn the meaningless malice of children wherever she had lived in her childhood, the circumstances of Janice's birth had drawn malice from her peers. Following the initial surprise and humiliation, what sweet relief it had been for Janice to know that she could not inherit this fatal disease from her mother. Mary's story was to be very different.

* * *

I married Mary in December, 1959, and first met her father six months later. The few days that we stopped close by his croft, carried no more significance than any other meeting of relatives who are brought together by marriage, except for one particular conversation. Whilst it was seven years since his wife's admission into hospital, it was a mere two since her death, and conversation had turned to her. I remember that it was a sunny day, and we were sitting outside on the grass. There was Mary, her brother's wife Judy, Judy's young children, and myself.

Mary's father muttered, "They're all rotten on that side of the family, they're all loony, they all end up in asylums". He then followed this by saying with pride and certainty, "It's not my side of the family, there's nothing wrong with us". Mary looked thoughtful, and Judy murmured assent.

This statement disturbed me and I never forgot it. If everyone in Mary's maternal family suffered from some kind of insanity, then perhaps it was hereditary. No, I reasoned, it must be hereditary, it could not be otherwise. It made me uneasy.

Mary's father slightly shocked me, with his crude, morally dismissive reference to Mary's mother and her family. Although it is stating the obvious, mental illness then, as now, induces fear and moral disapproval. I could hardly expect more from a man whom I had observed to be intelligent, but who, like a peasant, limited its direction towards cunning self-interest.

Over the following years, Mary worried that she might inherit this 'creeping paralysis'. We had no intention of having children, so there was no pressing reason to inquire into her maternal family history. Soon after our relationship had started, I insisted that she go to the Telford Road birth control clinic, one of the oldest to be established in Britain. Two years later, consequent upon our changing our address, she had transferred to a clinic in East Acton, where one of the doctors once criticized her for not having any children. Shortly afterwards I solved the problem, so that Mary no longer had to waste time attending clinics, nor to risk any further criticisms.

I heard of the Simon Population Trust, which put men who wished to be vasectomised in contact with surgeons practising the operation. I was informed that it would be necessary to follow current medical ethics and to obtain the consent of my general practitioner, in addition to filling in the inevitable forms.

I had a good relationship with my doctor. He was a kindly and courteous man, always calm and relaxed and prepared to visit sick people in their homes. He was the perfect family doctor. But, he was Irish and Catholic, a combination that I guessed would cause trouble when I asked for his permission to undergo the surgery.

My anticipation was justified, for on hearing my request this normally kind man was transformed from Jekyll to Hyde. He stiffened into an upright posture in his seat, and half rose from it, his face showing surprise and then anger as he peremptorily dismissed any possibility of giving his consent. He added that vasectomy was, "Sharp practice".

Alas, I have observed throughout my life that the precise codes of religion often perversely destroy the sympathetic awareness and kindness that can be found in the human race. I did not argue with him, there was no need to, because we were in Britain, not Southern Ireland. I had gone through the required form. The Simon Population Trust informed me, that

Catholic doctors, in particular, often refused to give their consent. I was duly referred to a surgeon, who performed the simple operation for me.

Mary was not alone in worrying, as the years passed, about this 'creeping paralysis'. Her sister-in-law, Judy, was also concerned. Judy had met Mary's brother, Jim, in the late 'forties, and they had produced four children between 1954 and 1960. Judy, therefore, had additional cause to worry because of the children. How much she knew of the medical history of her mother-in-law's family, I do not know. I do remember her assent when her father-in-law spoke about members of his wife's family ending in asylums. Perhaps it was only known to her by hearsay, and therefore was too tenuous to make a strong impression. Perhaps that first occasion, when I heard of other family members being afflicted by this scourge, was also the first time that Judy heard something definitive. I cannot believe that she would have borne children if she had known of a serious disease that they might inherit from Jim.

* * *

It was in 1970 that I first noticed slight chorea in Jim. He also started to become dull and listless. Jim was then 40 years old. I believed the symptoms to be the result of his hard labouring employment, with its weekly change of round-the-clock shifts. I did not see him often, so that each time we met I was able to note the progress of his decline. The chorea became worse, his mind slower. Additionally, his balance became poor, and increasingly he walked like someone who was 'drunk'. His speech became slurred and slow, and his facial expression vacuous. When he spoke, it was as if his thoughts came from a distance, as he slowly gathered them for utterance. After a few years of this slow deterioration, I began to doubt my original assumption that it was caused by his work.

Judy told Mary that Jim suspected he had the same disease as his mother. She frequently pressed him to see a doctor. "Perhaps", she would insist, "something could be done". Some intuitive doubt at the time made me sceptical.

In those years Jim would go to his doctor for common and trivial ailments, but never about his general condition. In retrospect, it is surprising that Dr Whiting allowed the situation to continue, for Jim was visibly ill and in need of the expert opinion of a neurologist. In addition, he saw no need to give any warning to the children, in spite of being informed of the family medical history by Judy. The children were adult or adolescent, and the eldest daughter made no secret of being sexually active, and therefore a potential child bearer.

It is more surprising that, if Jim believed his symptoms to be the same as his mother's, why this was not also recognized by Judy and Mary. Further, although Jim was seen by his father once, twice, or even three times annually throughout this period, he never mentioned that Jim had the same appearance or symptoms as his mother. Years later, when Jim's father did clearly state, in Mary's presence, that "Jim looks just like his mother", one denouement of the story that I am telling was about to take place, making his tardy observation unnecessary. His comment was too late to have any influence upon events, particularly in respect of warnings that should have been given to the children, especially the eldest. But, it was highly significant that, other than Jim's own belief that he had his mother's disease, it was the only admission from the four living family members who had seen her, that Jim's symptoms were, in fact, the same.

Throughout the early and middle 'seventies I was innocent in my ignorance. Never before had I seen anyone presenting the symptoms that Jim did. Neither Judy nor Mary appeared to recognize that they were similar to his mother's but, because Jim's father finally did state that they were the same, I was inclined to believe that both of them had been dishonest. I never challenged Judy on this vital issue, but Mary I did, and she always insisted, with obvious sincerity, that she could not remember

11

her mother's appearance. Is it possible that Mary's painful memories of her mother were so emotionally charged, that some were involuntarily blotted from her memory? But once more as so often when I consider these slowly unfolding events, my speculations remain unanswered.

* * *

It was during the late summer or autumn of 1977, that I first noticed that Mary had slight, very slight, involuntary movements of her arms. A stranger might not have noticed them. I did, because they were identical to the faint movements that Jim had shown years earlier. I was chilled. However, they were slight, and could not be compared with the pronounced chorea that Jim exhibited by that time. There was nothing else; she looked as normal and healthy as ever.

I thought that perhaps she reacted to stress in the same manner as her brother. She was a district nurse, and because of recent re-organisation of the domiciliary nursing service, she was even busier than normal. Previously, the nurses had worked within clearly defined areas, but recently they had been attached to individual doctors or groups of doctors, whose patients were spread over large areas, giving the nurses greater distances to travel. Demands, too, were made upon the nurses to produce more clerical records. These came from remote administrators, who presumably were justifying their newly-created posts. The nurses were also required to attend more meetings, and at some of these they were lectured on nursing topics, designed, no doubt, to create an ideal domiciliary service, but irrelevant to the realities that they faced each day.

District nursing does not have set working hours. A nurse stops when all her patients have been visited and her clerical work completed. Her hours fluctuate daily, because she must tend additional patients when her colleagues are sick or take leave. New patients are constantly given to her, so that her workload is determined daily, even hourly, by her supervisors, and in part by her colleagues, who must make quick arbitrary

12

decisions to meet the changes. If she does not have a personality of sufficient strength to defend her interests, she may be the recipient of arrangements which unfairly increase her weekly hours of work. The district nurse then, is subject to considerable stress.

This is how I rationalised away my fears. But Mary's twitching persisted, and it was identical to Jim's seven years ago, and it was whispered that he had his mother's disease, and Jim was Mary's brother. I said nothing to Mary; I feared to worry her unnecessarily, and for the moment, whilst the twitching was so slight, I was trying, ineffectually, to hide from the truth. In the future Mary was to comment frequently upon her family, and other people connected with the disease who did not react responsibly to it, with the words, "Brian, they are hiding".

* * *

Our life continued as before, there was nothing of note to disturb it, except for this twitching which would not go away. Neither would my concern, as I observed it every day. After a few months I could not remember clearly what Mary had looked like prior to that autumn. Perhaps she had always twitched slightly, and I had never before noticed it.

Christmas approached, and we were invited to spend Christmas Day with Jim and Judy, and their family. I decided that I must consult with Judy. She had not seen Mary during the past year. I would allow a few hours to pass, and then, during a suitable private moment, ask her if she saw anything unusual about Mary.

We arrived at their house in the afternoon. I was, for the first time, slightly sickened by Jim. He was obviously worse, but my new reaction was not because of this change. Previously he had lived in another family, another house, removed from Mary and me. He and his family had not been part of Mary's life with me. But now it was different, the link that had always existed was becoming tangible. I felt that Mary and I were being irresistibly pulled into a destructive vortex. Jim was a pitiful sight, but fear repelled me.

At a suitable moment I asked Judy for an opinion. I hoped, how I hoped, that she had noticed nothing, but she did not hesitate when I asked; she, too, had spotted Mary's slight involuntary twitching, she, too, recognized its similarity to that which Jim had shown several years earlier.

That evening, in such contrast to her brother, Mary had never appeared so soft, warm, and feminine, and now, in my eyes she possessed a childlike innocence and vulnerability because of what I knew I had to do.

* * *

Following the Christmas holiday I spoke gently to her about the twitching. I did not mention her brother. I did not relate her twitching to his condition. I asked her to see our doctor. Probably, I suggested, the cause was trivial, and could be easily explained. But I did not believe this, and it was obvious that Mary didn't either. She had not noticed these tiny jerks of her arms, and she was shaken and worried. At first she stubbornly refused to see him, but in the following months I frequently pressed her to make an appointment, until, finally, she agreed to go.

I anxiously awaited her return, confident that Dr Clement would either diagnose the cause of the twitching, or refer her to a hospital for a more detailed examination. When Mary returned, she explained that the consultation had been indeterminate. Dr Clement was away on holiday, and a young locum had seen her. She had told him everything that she knew about her family's medical history, and her own incipient chorea. He had been blandly reassuring. He had put an arm round her shoulders, and tried to allay her fear by telling her that she would not have her mother's disease. He made no examination.

I wanted to accept the locum's words, I wanted to believe in his soothing dismissal of our apprehension. I wanted to be rid of the constant worry that her chorea gave me. He was, after all, a qualified physician, he should know if anything was wrong. But I was not comforted, and neither was Mary. She was silent, and unwilling to discuss the matter further. I had prevailed upon her to see a doctor, so for the moment I said nothing more. It was as if we had declared an uneasy truce with a gross and menacing force, and could, temporarily at least, ignore it.

At the time, I believed that this young locum had been very unprofessional. Later that year my opinion of him changed. I suspect that he may have intentionally given Mary just a little more time. But I will never know.

Chapter 2

Following Christmas, other problems had arisen in our domestic life that caused tension and open strife between us. I found, for example, that I was doing most of the domestic chores. I knew that in many marriages the partners had distinctly separate duties that were usually aligned along the traditional male and female roles. Mary and I did not have a clear division. There were some areas that out of dislike we would leave the other to manage, but generally we were flexible, and each did what was needed as it arose. In the early months of 1978 I became responsible for most of the shopping, the housework, the garden care, and walking the dog. This was because her nursing duties were taking progressively more of her time.

It was true, that because of the changes I have described above, she had more work than before. This was confirmed by one of her nursing friends, who took early retirement that year, because she was unwilling to tolerate the additional work and stress. Later in that summer, a nursing auxiliary who had worked with Mary, was sent to hospital, suffering from exhaustion.

In the early months of 1978 Mary frequently worked through the evenings on patients' record cards, and other clerical tasks, following a full day's nursing. I reacted to this by pressing her to leave the nursing service, and to look for less demanding work elsewhere with reasonable hours. I took to searching the local newspaper's situations vacant columns, drawing her attention to possible openings. But she was unwilling to make any move. Faced with this obduracy, I often became angry and abusive towards her.

I also pressed her to claim payment for the hours that she worked in excess of those for which she was paid. These would be unusual claims in the nursing service, and she was most reluctant to make them, but she submitted, after constant bullying pressure from me. I reasoned, that it was more important to make her supervisors aware that she was working long hours, than to receive payment for them.

Some payments were made, and then in later months it was agreed to give her time off in lieu of the overtime. She did not receive all that was due to her. Some payments were arbitrarily withheld, and she took very little time off. I kept a record of her working hours, and I was scrupulously correct with my entries. Looking back, I now see that this put stress upon me, and caused Mary humiliation, as I daily asked for details from her.

She worked at her record cards until midnight, on each of the three days preceding our annual holiday in May. It was normal for me to take the major share of holiday preparations, but that year I did everything. I was tired and angry, and whilst waiting for our flight at Heathrow, I demanded a promise from her that she would leave the nursing service. I did not feel that I could relax and enjoy the holiday unless I knew that she would do this on our return. It led to a frightful row in public, which ended when Mary smashed a glass ash-ray down on to the table where we sat. Faced with this, I fell silent. I was baffled and angry. The problem remained unresolved.

In spite of the unpropitious start, we enjoyed this holiday in North America. Away from the relentless demands of her work, Mary was cheerful and relaxed; I realised how tired and depressed she had been in the previous months. Even her twitching decreased.

Our marriage had been eroded, and I was worried that it would break down in the future, but I continued to hope that I could persuade Mary to retire from nursing.

On our return all the pre holiday stresses were immediately re-established. Before 8.00 a.m. on her first working day the telephone rang. It was a nursing colleague forcefully pressing the day's work on to her. Mary was back once more on the treadmill, rushing about during the days, and poring over her record cards in the evenings. Burdened as before with all the domestic responsibilities, I resumed my unrelenting pressure upon her to stop nursing. All the strife between us returned.

* * *

In that summer of 1978 her involuntary arm movements became worse. They could no longer be ignored. I observed that, during sleep, Mary was perfectly still. Surely then, I thought, the chorea must be due to stress? It was also in those post holiday months that I first sensed something bland and unresponsive in her personality. It was not the stubbornness to which I was accustomed, rather, it was as if she was unable to react decisively to situations. She appeared to be constantly, albeit slightly, dazed.

At that time, Mary always rejected my direct appeals for her to see our doctor about the chorea, but in September an opportunity arose, and I grasped it. We both had to see him because of rashes that we had developed simultaneously. As we drove to the surgery, I suggested that we should speak to him about her twitching. She quietly agreed. Once in his surgery the rashes were quickly dealt with and I went straight on to tell him about Mary's chorea, and everything that we knew of her family's medical history. His reaction was very different from that of the locum. He asked a few questions. One that I remember, was whether she had double vision. (That would be a symptom of multiple sclerosis). However, he was unable to come to any conclusion, and he arranged for Mary to see a neurologist.

In the following week Mary developed influenza, but Dr Clement did not send her back to work when she recovered. He continued to give her certificates, changing the entry on them to 'involuntary movements'.

I had been forcefully pressing Mary to see a doctor for months and she had suddenly agreed. It had been like beating at a door that unexpectedly opens to reveal a dark interior without the safety of familiar dimensions. In the future that dark interior was to be far more fearful than I had imagined. As we waited for Mary's appointment with the neurologist, we sensed that we were trapped. The past, with its whispers and half truths, had suddenly moved across space and time, and was about to engulf us.

* * *

Meanwhile, there took place another of the coincidences that feature from time to time in this story. Judy had been told of Mary's hospital appointment. She knew that its result would be vital for the future of herself, and Jim, and their four children. But unexpectedly, just one week before the appointment, an ambulance had been called by Jim's employer to take him for medical examination direct to hospital, to the same department where Mary was due to go.

Jim was obviously a sick man, with symptoms that stretched back for eight years, so it was surprising nothing similar had happened before. Throughout those years he continued to drive the family car, and to ride a moped to work. A year or two earlier he had been stopped by police who were doing random roadworthy tests on vehicles. They had quickly lost interest in his moped, and turned to him, in the belief that he was 'drunk'. Jim had been given a breathaliser test which had been negative, and the police, in their ignorance, had been obliged to allow him to ride away.

During the intervening week, Mary was silent and tense. We both were frightened. The last night before the appointment I did an uncharacteristic thing; I begged her not to go. I knew that it would only confirm the worst that we feared.

The appointment time was 2.00 p.m., but Mary did not return until 7.00 p.m.. She was distraught, weeping intermittently, and shaking. I was desperately anxious to hear what had happened, but had difficulty getting a coherent account of the day's events out of her.

She told me that on her arrival at the hospital, they had been waiting for her. Jim had said that his sister would be there in the following week. Without this disclosure of the sibling relationship, a correct diagnosis of Mary would not have been easy. She had found this reception humiliating, for she sensed, probably correctly, that they had half decided upon the diagnosis before her arrival. She was asked to do various physical movements, and was then asked questions such as, "Who is the Prime Minister" and, "Where do you live". Next, she did simple arithmetic for them; addition and subtraction.

It all seemed quite strange to me. She was not examined in any way that I would call scientific. Even with all the knowledge that I have now, several years later, I am not surprised that at the time I failed to grasp the implications of their questions. They were asked in a random manner, and, as a test of an individual's intellectual capabilities, were witless and without method. I felt a little optimistic as she told me about it. It seemed to be farcical that, in the scientific twentieth century, this was the best that they could do. I began to think that perhaps, after all, little was wrong with Mary. But then, right at the end the blow came, and my fear returned undiminished. They had told Mary before she left, that she had the same disease as her brother.

In a shocked state, Mary had taken the wrong tube train. She told me that before getting into it she had thought of throwing herself on to the line in front, as it approached. She had alighted at the wrong station, where she had been spotted by the daughter of an ex-patient. This lady, seeing Mary rolling and stumbling, at first thought that she was 'drunk', and had taken her to her home, which was nearby. She had kept Mary there for an hour or two until she was in a calmer state, and had then driven her home to me.

Two more weeks passed before Dr Clement received Mary's file from the hospital. We went together to his surgery but when our turn came he, looking ill-at-ease, hesitated, then asked us to go in separately. Mary was first. A few minutes later it was my turn, and as I followed him into the surgery I remembered that many years ago, when my dog had been given urgent surgery, the veterinary surgeon had taken me aside to break the news that he had died. He, too, I remembered, had looked ill-at-ease because of what he had to impart to me. We seated ourselves, he looking away.

Then diffidently and clumsily, he said, "I'm sorry the news is not good over your wife, she has a form of chorea". Hardly had he finished when it came to me intuitively, "Its Huntington's", I said. He nodded assent.

For a few seconds my mind raced in turmoil. I knew that my life had ended. At that moment, I was returned to my normal experience of constant anxiety and fear, remission coming only during sleep. I was back to my old struggle to retain a rational control of my emotions, barely able to survive. The years that I had lived in London, which had seemed to be permanent, had been a mere interlude. This time, unlike earlier desperate periods, I had been thrust into a situation from which I believed I had no chance to escape. It stretched before me and I felt helpless and frightened. I knew in those few seconds, that I would no longer be able to tolerate the superficial relationships with other people that pass as normal. I would be unable to continue deferring to the unreal social norms that surrounded me. In those two or three seconds I plunged into despair, knowing that there was not the slightest possibility that I would be able to support Mary as she deteriorated. Our lives would become messy and sordid. Why should a problem of such magnitude have come to us? Why me? I was so ill equipped to cope with it.

"But what of my wife", I said to Dr Clement, "What shall I tell her?"

He had told her no more than me, and she had not chosen to question him. We both knew it was a metaphorical question. He looked helpless, and slowly shook his head.

21

* * *

When we returned home Mary was withdrawn and pale, I could not imagine what she was experiencing. She knew that her life was now at an end, that there was no escape for her. It was enough, no, it was more than enough for her to know that she had the disease which had killed her mother. She could not cope with anything more, although I knew that eventually she would learn the truth, that she had the dreaded Huntington's chorea.

I remembered that a few years earlier Mary had nursed a patient with the disease. Before its onset this patient, too, had been a nurse. The disease had been in an advanced stage. This patient could barely speak and was not easily understood. She could not stand unaided. She had to be hand fed, and she was doubly incontinent. Mary visited her regularly, and on some days she would arrive when the patient's friend, who was caring for her, had dashed out to shop. On those days, Mary sometimes found her patient lying on the floor, having fallen out of bed because of her violent choreic movements. She would be unable to rise, and perhaps surrounded by her faeces. The friend could not really manage, but she had taken the patient out of hospital because she had not been given basic nursing care. She had been left to lie in a cot, so, in addition to all the advanced symptoms of the disease, she had many pressure sores. The Superintendent of District Nurses had been so shocked by this patient's condition that she had unprecedentedly arranged for photographs to be taken of her, to use as evidence in action she intended to take against the hospital.

As a district nurse, Mary's work was predominantly with the elderly. Therefore, many of her patients did not recover; either they died, or they entered geriatric units. It was quite unlike the relatively high recovery rate of patients in hospital surgical wards.

Mary sometimes talked to me about cases if they were particularly sad or unusual. I remember that at the time, she said that this patient with Huntington's chorea was the worst she had ever nursed. On hearing the details from her, I had agreed. Here, again, was yet another of the coincidences that occur in this story. Mary was destined to fall victim to the very disease that, in its horror, had impressed her more than any other. She was doomed to succumb to it, and she had been, from the moment of her conception.

* * *

Huntington's chorea is eponymously named after an American doctor, George Huntington, who wrote the first definitive paper on it in 1872. His work was soon translated into a number of Western languages, which ensured that there was widespread knowledge of the disease before the end of the nineteenth century. It is an hereditary disease that is caused by an auto sominal dominant gene. This means that for every baby conceived having a parent carrying the gene, there is a one in two chance that the gene, and thus the disease, will be inherited. It a thousand babies have a parent with the gene, between four hundred and fifty and five hundred and fifty, for example, will inherit it. At some time during the life of those who inherit the gene, the disease will become manifest. This can happen at any age. The average is forty years. It cannot cross generations, but only appears to do so if a carrier of the gene should, after procreating, die before the disease has broken out. There is no means of knowing who is carrying the gene, because at the moment predictive tests are not available. It is only when people at risk reach the age of seventy or eighty, that there is reasonable certainty that they did not inherit the gene from the affected parent.

The disease is invariably fatal. Its duration from the manifest inception until the individual's death, averages fifteen years. The younger or older the victims are at the onset of the disease, the shorter their life expectancy is likely to be. Some sufferers will live well over twenty years, others less than five, but this latter circumstance is very rare, unless death is caused by suicide or causes not directly related to the disease. With few exceptions, victims are committed to mental institutions at some time during the progress of the disease. They may be incarcerated for years before death releases them.

The origin of the disease is obscure, but it is reasonable to believe, even certain, that at some time in the past millennia one person suffered a genetical mutation. As populations have grown and spread around the world, so the fatal gene, and hence the disease, has also spread. It is prevalent in white Caucasian populations, and in local populations which have interbred with them. It is rare or non-existent where there has not been interbreeding with whites. Thus, in the United States, it has the normal prevalence rates in whites that is found in people of European origin, but the blacks have a much lower rate, and in black Africa it seems to be almost non-existent. It seems, then, to have originated in Europe, and a study of population movements and prevalence rates of the disease today, indicates North Western Europe.

It is believed by some people that, when Huntington's chorea becomes manifest in an individual from a family where there is no history of the disease, a fresh mutation has taken place. This is very unlikely. The geographical spread clearly points to Europe as the area from which the disease started. If mutations continue to occur, one would expect to find the disease endemic throughout the world. Because this is not the case, unless white Caucasians have a distinct and special disposition to repeat the mutation occasionally, then these apparent mutations must be due to illegitimacy, adoption, or late onset in consecutive generations.

The pathology of the disease consists of the progressive atrophy of cells of the brain. The cardinal areas affected are the cerebral cortex and basal ganglia. The chorea that is associated with 90% of affected individuals is believed to be caused by basal ganglia dysfunction. It is clear from the latest research that the human brain is controlled by complex chemical processes. The mutant gene causing Huntington's chorea effectively upsets these, and cells in parts of the brain die at an accelerated rate.

Symptoms vary between individuals in type, severity, and time of onset, and both mind and body are affected. The most common physical symptom suffered by victims, and probably the first to be clearly manifest, is chorea. Generally, it starts with slight twitching or jerking, but progresses to become gross, before reducing in the late stages of the disease. It always stops during sleep. Gait is always affected. In the 90% who are choreic, it is characteristically swaying, tripping, changing in speed, and irregular in direction. In the 10% who are rigid it is slow, with head bent forward. Falls, with subsequent fractures or lacerations, are common. Many victims are unable to walk unaided. Speech is always affected. It may at first be merely slurred, but later it can become incomprehensible. Many victims have difficulty in swallowing during the advanced stages, and this is often the cause of death, when food or drink enters the trachea and causes infection of the lungs. 80% have eye dysfunction. They are unable to move their eyes rapidly from side to side. Thus, the characteristic rolling of the eyes becomes apparent. Most victims lose weight, some excessively. This could be the result of insufficient food to offset the energy loss caused by the chorea. It could also follow from loss of appetite in a patient, due to depression. Most people with the disease look older than their actual years. 20% become doubly incontinent, usually in the later stages. Epilepsy is rather more common than average amongst patients.

Turning to the effect of Huntington's chorea upon the mind, the symptoms are no less dreadful, and for the victim's spouse or family, they are probably more alarming. They are more difficult to define clinically. It has been suggested that there is a parallel between them and the symptoms of normal senile decay, but whilst this may be a useful introductory guide for the layman, it is too crude for people who are closely involved with the disease. One can generalise and say that progressive dementia is characteristic of all victims, but use of the word 'dementia' probably reveals that its user is unable to define the mental symptoms with any precision.

It is certain that affected people progressively decline in their intellectual capabilities. Their memories deteriorate, and they lose the ability to be decisive and positive. Their conceptual thought becomes slow and impaired. Invariably there are personality changes that may be subtle or well defined. Schizophrenic psychosis is more common than average. Depression is a very common symptom, but it is not clear how much can be attributed to the changes brought about directly by the biological damage to the brain, and how much is the very natural consequence of victims' awareness of their condition and its prognosis.

Recent research in hitherto neglected fields has revealed that the crime rate, both petty and serious, in people suffering from Huntington's chorea, is higher than average. It is not yet known whether this is a direct result of the disease upon victims' minds, or a result of the disturbed social conditions in which they are likely to be living. There is, too, a higher than average death rate amongst unaffected children in Huntington families, which points to neglect and ill-treatment. Not surprisingly, alcoholism is higher than average amongst the disease's victims, and it is probable that nicotine addiction is, too.

The prevalence of Huntington's chorea in white Caucasian populations is generally agreed to be between 30 and 70 people per million. In Britain the official Ministry of Health figure for known affected people is 4,000, but it is estimated that the true figure is 6,000, with 30,000 people at risk, whilst the total number of people directly involved, including those who have married into affected families, is estimated to be 50,000. The apparent inbalance between the figures for those suffering from the disease and those at risk to it arises, because the number of related grandchildren, nieces and nephews, must be added to the number of direct progeny of affected individuals, to gain a true figure of the total number at risk.

In 1977 an estimate was made of the financial cost of people with

Huntington's chorea in the U.S.A.. The figure varied from $65,000 to $234,000 per patient. Similar estimates were computed in Britain, which gave a figure of £20,000, and in South Africa, where the figure was R28,000. The total direct annual cost of Huntington's chorea in the U.S.A. is estimated to be from $110 to $125 million. In 1980, the National Health Service was estimated to spend £4 million annually on the caring services for victims of the disease. All these figures are minimum, and they do not include the loss of the productive skills of victims, or those family members caring for them to the state. Nor do they include the loss of earnings to afflicted individuals and to the spouse or other relatives caring for them, which often reduces whole families to penury.

Perhaps the most striking statistic of Huntington's chorea is the suicide rate. Suicide is most frequent in the early stages of the disease. It is reasonable to presume that this is because of the will and organisation that is needed for a successful suicide, which an advanced patient would not have. Another factor must be the additional, even insuperable, difficulties for would-be suicides who are incarcerated in mental hospitals. The rate varies between countries, and it is modified by national suicide rates. It is seven to two hundred times greater than average!

* * *

Within two days of being told by Dr Clement that Mary had Huntington's chorea, I telephoned my sister-in-law, Judy. I considered that it would be more satisfactory to speak to her in isolation from her family and from Mary, to discuss the situation that we shared, so I used a public call-box and dialled her office. I anticipated that she would be no less horrified than I was by the diagnosis. In addition, there was the dreadful dimension that all her four children were at a one-in-two risk of having inherited the disease. In those early days I was in a constant state of excitement, so I did not waste any time with conventional pleasantries.

"You've heard, of course, what it is?" I asked immediately.

"No", she replied.

"Hasn't your doctor had the papers from the hospital then?" I asked with surprise, because Jim was there one week before Mary.

"Oh yes", said Judy, "we've been to see him. He said that the hospital are writing to Scotland".

Then from me, and spoken with incredulity, "Didn't he tell you what it was then?"

"No", she replied.

I was astonished. I could not know then, that it was to be the first of many times that I was to react with some measure of surprise to the moral pusillanimity of people involved with the disease. This doctor was new to the family, for they had moved to another address in the previous year, but his lack of moral responsibility in view of the information that he had received from the hospital, was even more pronounced than Whiting's.

I gave no more time towards establishing just how informed Judy was, and spoke straight out. "It's Huntington's chorea".

I heard her gasp, she had once worked for a time at St. Giles. She must have heard of the disease.

I went straight on, "You'll have to tell the children, they should be sterilised, of course".

They ranged in age from 18 to 24, but I sensed that she would do nothing; that she would avoid informing them.

She said something about the disease passing only through the female line.

"No", I explained, "genetically the sex of a parent makes no difference, it can be inherited from either one".

I remember that at the time her pitiful search for reassurance meant nothing to me, and I resented the indifference towards Mary in favour of concern for her children that it implied.

That call was the first of many that I was to make from public boxes in the ensuing months. No more would be made to Judy, but with few exceptions, telephone calls to other people would similarly increase rather than diminish my loneliness, because of the gulf that they revealed between my definitive reaction to the disease, and the moral ambivalence shown by other people.

One week later I called to see Judy's youngest daughter at her place of work. I asked if she had been told what afflicted her father. She said she had not. I had been correct, then, in believing that Judy would remain silent and not warn the children. It seemed incredible to me at the time. I was in a wildly excited state and lacked any sensitive tact in my manner.

Abruptly, I told her that Jim suffered from Huntington's chorea, and went on to explain the hereditary factor. I emphasized that she must warn her three siblings, for it was imperative that none of them should have children.

To my surprise Catrina appeared to be indifferent to my news. My ebullient state did not stop me from resenting this apparent absence of concern. However, she did promise to contact her brother and two sisters.

A year later, her eldest sister criticised me for informing Catrina so impetuously. I defended myself by explaining that, at that time, I was faced with the emerging revelation that the disease was surrounded by a conspiracy of silence. Horrified as I was with Mary's prognosis, my immediate concern in reacting to this conspiracy, was to ensure that Jim's children knew that they must not procreate, so that no more lives would be wrecked in the future.

It is my belief that other people were relieved that I informed Catrina. It took the responsibility for doing so away from them, but at the time, this thought never occurred to me.

* * *

In those early days following the diagnosis, Mary told me what she could remember of her maternal relatives. It was very little. She recalled that when she was a small child, her grandmother always seemed to be in bed. This in itself did not prove that the grandmother suffered from the disease, and was therefore the parent who passed the gene to Mary's mother. Mary could not remember her grandfather, so it was equally possible that he was the carrier, and that the disease had claimed him before Mary's childhood.

Mary's grandparents had five children. The eldest, James, died in hospital in 1967. I have estimated his age to be close to 70. He was unmarried. The second son, George, who was the father of two children, was unaffected when Mary last saw him at her mother's funeral. There were three daughters. The eldest died before Mary's mother. She was unmarried. Mary clearly remembered that the youngest sister, whilst still in her thirties, was always in a wheelchair. She, too, was unmarried.

It is reasonable to believe, that this sister had inherited the fatal gene. It is also possible that the early death of the eldest sister was caused by the disease. James is uncertain, and George also, because he may have developed the disease after 1958. Following that year, all contact was lost between the various members of the family. Most interesting of all, only two of the five siblings married. Could the others have chosen to remain single because of the frightful disease that had afflicted past generations of their family?

I thought once more of Mary's father's statement, "They're all rotten on that side of the family". I remembered my first wife's parents who had adopted Janice. I thought of Mary's mother, who, after deteriorating for many years at home, had still to endure five more long years in hospital before dying. I ruminated on the many generations of unknown people stretching back in time, whose lives had been ruined by Huntington's chorea. I thought of the permutations of suffering that the disease must have brought; of the many times individuals, for example, had been burdened with a succession of relatives to nurse; perhaps a parent, a sibling, a nephew or niece, spread over many decades. I thought of the consequences when husbands were stricken with the disease in past centuries. How many had slowly lost control of their craft or profession, as their minds were stealthily eroded? I thought of the ignorance and fear with which the disease had been regarded, and the resulting hostility towards affected families and individuals, which in some cases had led to accusations of witchcraft against them.

I came back sharply to the present, and was sickened by fear and despair as I looked at Mary. It was unnecessary to marvel on the suffering of others, because Mary and I had our own sorrow. We had become part of that historical vista.

* * *

One month following Mary's diagnosis, I arranged to meet the Registrar who had made it. Dr. Field was a youngish, genial man, and we talked for forty-five minutes. He spoke about Mary and Jim, and he said that he was "ninety-eight per cent sure" that it was Huntington's chorea which afflicted them, but he had written off to Scotland for information on their mother. He continued by saying that Mary would never nurse again and must no longer drive a car.

I was frank with him about my own inability to cope. The difficulties of the past year, when Mary had been in the initial stages of the disease, presaged what I feared would follow. I mentioned that I could not understand why I had failed to connect other more sinister symptoms shown by Mary, with the obvious chorea.

He self deprecatingly replied, that doctors were no better than lay people at spotting pathological symptoms in their own family members. He then surprised me by saying that with the present shortage of beds, he could not admit Mary to hospital.

I had not even hinted at such a possibility. It seemed wildly irrelevant and unnecessary, because the disease was plainly embryonic in Mary.

He continued by estimating that she would have to enter hospital in about three years' time, and that meanwhile there would be difficulties. I would, of course, be able to receive the assistance of various social services. There would be, for example, the soiled linen service when Mary became incontinent. He added to this, that, as the disease progressed, Mary would cease to care or worry about her condition.

At that time I knew less about Huntington's chorea than I do now, but I did know that its progression was slow, and I had observed this to be the case with Mary's brother. Three years was a grossly misleading underestimate of the probable period before Mary would have to enter hospital. I also knew that it was quite incorrect to assume that even advanced victims of the disease are indifferent to their fate.

I said nothing in reply to these statements by Dr. Field. Instead, I introduced another topic.

"My wife and I do not have children", I explained, "but my brother-in-law has four, and all of them are adults. You should see them very soon and arrange for their sterilisation".

I remember that he screwed up his face quizzically at this and said, "Well it is difficult, there is only a fifty per cent chance that they will get it".

My chest tightened and my heart beat rapidly. It was the first of many occasions that I was confronted by a person who held the opinions that were responsible for the catastrophe that had struck Mary and me.

Field had not bothered to ask Jim or Mary if they had children. In the weeks between his diagnosis of Jim, and my visit, my nephew Roy could have been sexually involved with a promiscuous girl. She could have become pregnant, not knowing who the father was. Her child could have been a grandparent before the disease became manifest, should the mutant gene have been passed on.

This interview with Field further confirmed why Huntington's chorea existed more than a century after the first definitive paper had been written about it. It was not only lay ignorance, but professional irresponsibility, that ensured its continuing transmission. Whatever it had been named in Scotland, it was patent that the disease was hereditary. No warning had been given to Mary or to Jim, nor presumably to their father. Worse, Field, having made a diagnosis, had done nothing to warn the people at risk, and neither had Judy's G.P.. It was an insane conspiracy of silence, but in the years that followed I would be considered unbalanced because of my natural rage in reaction to it. I would also be criticised for my inability to cope with a situation that I had not created, and which was not accidental.

In the days following my interview with Field, I pondered upon his statements that Mary would have to enter hospital within three years, and that victims of the disease become indifferent to their condition. As a neurologist, it did not seem possible that he could be so ignorant in his own field. Could it be, I asked myself, that observing my fear he had attempted to allay it with expedient statements? He must had known that Mary and I faced immense suffering over a lengthy period of perhaps fifteen or twenty years. Did he think it desirable to assuage, temporarily, my present trepidation whilst being indifferent, even ambivalent, towards the vital need to stop the transmission of the disease that caused such suffering? Why, if he evinced such callous indifference towards eliminating Huntington's chorea, did he quite fairly and responsibly tell me that Mary should no longer be allowed to drive?

In those early days I was constantly reeling under the fearful blows of the moral inconsistencies underlying other people's reactions to the disease. It often seemed that these people had access to information of which I was ignorant, and that their assumptions had a rational base. I was to clash angrily with people who believed that it was the right of everyone to have children whatever the result. I was to brush against apparently normal people whose opinions and actions were part of a syndrome of gross irresponsibility that ensured the survival of Huntington's chorea, with all its misery. Not one of them would have to bear the consequences of their opinions.

Chapter 3

I find it as impossible now, as I did throughout the years following, to comprehend the total lack of hope that Mary must have felt from the day that she was diagnosed. Neither of us at any time mentioned the possibility of a cure, or a drug that might slow down the deterioration. The hospital had given her tetrabenzine. This could, as Field claimed in a callowly enthusiastic manner, "stiffen them up".

In Mary's case it produced somnolence, and it was entirely unnecessary since her chorea was not pronounced then, and never was, in the following years. She took the drug for one day only, almost as a child will innocently obey orders, safe in the belief that authority knows best. I heard later than this drug, never intended to be more than a palliative, had no effect whatsoever upon her brother Jim's chorea.

Daily she faced the fearful fact that her body and mind were slowly dying. As a nurse she had no illusions, for she had frequently witnessed the degrading features of many illnesses. In her domiciliary work she had observed the havoc to family relationships that chronic illness can bring.

Although for the moment she was technically still employed, and would be for one more year until her sick leave ended, practically, her working life had ended at the premature age of 47. I had never taken her job seriously. I had always regarded it to be like my own, a necessary but unrewarding daily chore. It was in those early days following the diagnosis, that I first became aware of how important nursing had been to Mary. During the years of our marriage, the unfair and exacting conditions governing the work had precluded me from recognizing her marked vocation for nursing the elderly. Every supervisor, since she started district nursing, had remarked upon the warm relationships that she formed with her patients. I remember, for example, that a year after the diagnosis when we were on holiday in a remote part of Lesotho, I was touched when we met a very aged and mellow African, and she had immediately warmed to him, and

35

hugged him, and held his face gently between her hands.

Quite abruptly, then, she was cut off from her patients without any warning, or the foreknowledge that a normal retirement would give. She often spoke bitterly of this in those early days. She found it frustrating and humiliating to be reduced, as she saw it, to the useless level of a housewife. In the years that followed, boredom was to be one of the dominant features of her life. The steady atrophy of her brain cells reduced the initiative that she needed to create fresh interests, and the clear knowledge of her hopeless situation caused depression which furthered the erosion of initiative. When she most needed the stimuli of contact with other people, it was denied to her. Friends, colleagues, neighbours, either never came to her aid from the start, or stopped doing so as the years passed.

During this early period, I did everything necessary to ensure that Mary was not told specifically that she had Huntington's chorea. She had not questioned Dr Clement's 'a form of chorea'. It was reasonable that she preferred to remain ignorant. She did not clearly know, as I did, that the disease that afflicted her was princely. I was aware that few could equal it in both horror and length, and that we were merely in the foothills of a vast mountain of suffering that would have to be climbed, before her inevitable death. She vaguely believed that she did not have many years to live. She did not appear to remember what I could infer, that her mother must have started to deteriorate before reaching the age of forty.

Every day I fearfully watched her for new symptoms. I was particularly frightened of mental deterioration. Constantly, I held the image in my mind of the patient she had nursed a few years earlier.

Her stoical courage was obvious, but my own lonely fear made me doubt what I could plainly see. The burden of the knowledge that I carried caused her own suffering to be diminished in my eyes. I began to resent her seeming innocence, and this resentment was fuelled by other factors stemming directly from the symptoms of the disease.

* * *

Immediately following Mary's diagnosis, my awareness of these symptoms came in a rush. In retrospect, I was surprised that I had failed to notice a number of changes, or to appreciate the significance of those I had seen. During the previous winter of 1977-78, for example, we had been to several ballroom dances where she seemed to be stiff and awkward in her movements. I had also been irritated by her manner of gripping my right shoulder in her left hand, pulling down constantly and heavily. I mentioned this to her at the time, but she had not responded by relaxing her hold. When we returned home following one dance, I had criticised her for it, and this had led to a row. We never went ballroom dancing again.

When walking alongside Mary, she was incapable of taking a precisely parallel course. It was subtle, but noticeable, that she gently bumped me with her shoulder. She also stumbled slightly as she walked. Her balance was poor, for when standing on firm ground she gave the impression that she was on the deck of a ship at sea, as she constantly shifted her feet in order to remain upright. She tended to roll her head on her shoulders, either backwards or forwards.

The chorea, which was the one symptom that I had not failed to recognise, was not gross. It was a general twitching and jerkiness affecting her face and limbs. It increased markedly when she was under stress, but when she was asleep she was quite still. I was told by a psychiatric nurse friend, that normal practice in hospitals is to wait until patients are asleep before covering them, otherwise it is likely that their choreaform movements will displace the blankets.

The most frightening symptoms were those that reflected the damage to her mind. She had been a fast reader and normally she read at twice my speed, but she had become slower even than I. Her writing was laboured, like that of a child. She could not organise her day, for she had

37

no method. She lacked the initiative to undertake new and unfamiliar tasks. She could not respond quickly to new situations. She was forgetful. As early as the spring of 1978 she caused me frequent irritation when she forgot to flush the toilet.

Although these many symptoms were painful and frightening, I was most affected by a quality of bland passivity that steadily increased to replace her normal, almost vivacious personality. Unlike so many of the disease's victims who become contrary and paranoid, Mary slowly, very slowly, began to lose some of the sharp contours of her personality to which I was accustomed. It was not that she was becoming overall feeble minded; it was more subtle than that. Her essential common sense, integrity, and wisdom, were unchanged, and were to remain unchanged, but more peripheral qualities were slowly fading. It was this change of personality, and the consequent loss of support, that previously she had afforded me, which I found most difficult to accept.

I wanted, in truth I needed, to be frank with her to discuss my fears, but I found it impossible to do so. I was inhibited by my wish not to disclose to her that she had Huntington's chorea, and my related concern that I had no right to burden her with any suggestion that she was becoming inadequate as my wife. Not only was I faced daily with her deterioration, but also for the first time since our relationship had developed nearly twenty years earlier, I was not able to communicate with her on an intimate level. I knew, too, that these contemporary difficulties affecting communication, would in time become irrelevant, because ultimately she would become incapable of any sensitive exchange of intimacies.

In those early months, the time scale of the disease was also dominant in my thoughts. The number of years that the disease would progress in an individual from its inception until death was uncertain, but it averaged fifteen. I was then forty six years old, so I could expect to be released from my responsibility only when I was near, or had reached, retirement. Without question, I knew that I could not cope for such a protracted period.

Five years, perhaps, but not ten, fifteen, or twenty.

Daily I was horrified by all the symptoms that did not remain static, but inexorably increased in severity. Like a ratcheted wheel that at best remains still and never can move in a reverse direction, Mary only halted temporarily in her decline. These symptoms, the genetic transmission and society's indifference, all conjoined to give me a feeling of disbelief that they were real. Not since I was a child and learning with incredulity that life was unlimited in its cruelty to man and beast, had I felt quite the same.

* * *

My reactions to her were at times very cruel and unfair. It is insufficient to recognise one's own shortcomings, or more specifically, one's own infantile regressions. Awareness of a broken leg does not mend it. At best, one attempts to walk using crutches, but there were none available to me in those early days and in the years that followed. Like a rejected child, I frequently could not bring myself to respond to the love that she always gave me. It was changing steadily to become more like the love of a child rather than a woman, and it was not enough for me.

There were times, when with passionately angry voice, I accused her of allowing me to be drawn into marriage. Why, I asked, had she done nothing to inquire into her family's history? Surely I would add, she must have known something, if, as her father had said, so many ended in mental hospitals. Most cruel of all because of its element of truth, I would say that I would not have left a stone unturned to lay bare my own family's medical history in similar circumstances. Had I known what she was at risk to, I would have broken off the incipient relationship in the weeks following our meeting, before bonding could have taken place.

And so, from the very beginning, two or three times every week, my frustration and fear, and my rage with the society that had casually allowed, and continues to allow, the transmission of Huntington's chorea, led to regular crises in which Mary was the recipient of my venom. Just when she most needed love and support she received anger from me. This pattern, which was established soon after her diagnosis, was to continue for the next two and a half years. Except for short periods during holidays, it lasted until I was given the supportive 'crutches' that I desperately needed.

* * *

Huntington's chorea has two primary features. One of them is the long and progressive deterioration of affected individuals eventually leading to their deaths, and the other is the hereditary nature of its transmission. It is generally accepted to be an appalling disease hardly exceeded by any other in the suffering that it causes, while the mode of its transmission adds quite exceptional social and personal ramifications, which frequently lead to the destruction of family relationships.

From the moment that Mary was diagnosed, and subsequent inquiries gave me the salient facts about the disease, one of my first reactions was surprise that more than a century after George Huntington's paper had been published, the disease continued to be transmitted. I was later to learn from the Secretary of State for Health, 'That the number of observed and projected new cases in patients born between 1900-1970 has remained almost constant despite a progressive reduction in birth rate in the general population during this period in Britain'. It was axiomatic to me then, and has been so ever since, to believe that the disease should have been eliminated from Britain and other developed countries long ago, by the simple means of stopping all people at risk from breeding. I was to learn in those early days that my simple rational humanism, if not unique, was unusual. At times in my lonely frustration, it seemed to me to be rare.

There are only two ways in which Huntington's chorea can be eliminated, either by basic bio-chemical research, or by tracing all choreics and those at risk, and putting them into custody until they agree to be sterilised. The former means has been unsuccessful and it is likely to remain so. The brain is now known to be controlled by complex chemical processes, and a cure for the disease may only be found many years in the future, and the research would be very costly. The latter means is practical and possible in all developed countries.

In the United Kingdom there are twenty five notifiable diseases. Alphabetically, they range from Acute Encephalitis to Yellow Fever. Legislation exists empowering health authorities to control the spread of these diseases: 'A justice of the peace may, on the application of a local authority, order the removal of an infectious patient to hospital, and may order his detention therein'. A famous example of a modern state doing this occurred, when New York kept Mary Mallou, known as 'Typhoid Mary', a carrier of the disease, in detention from 1915 until her death in 1938.

In addition, there are the mental health acts, which similarly enable authority to incarcerate people, judged to be dangerous to themselves or to others, in mental institutions, if necessary for life!

By contrast, those suffering from Huntington's chorea, and those at risk to it, are allowed to transmit the disease by procreating. Why should such double standards exist? The answer is simple. Although Huntington's chorea is as frightful as any notifiable disease, it is genetic in transmission, so it is limited to families carrying the mutant gene. The other reason is that future victims are unborn and therefore unable to protest. If the disease were infectious the public clamour arising would long ago have resulted in firm action for its elimination. We are left with the simple fact, that the disease flourishes more than a century after George Huntington wrote his paper, because of selfish lack of concern for future victims on the part of successive Ministers for Health, Members of Parliament, doctors, the general public, and above all by those either with the disease or at risk from it, who breed.

* * *

In addition to the fear and despair that had suddenly fallen upon us, there arose practical problems that needed my attention. I knew that Mary would never work again, and that she would receive a pension and possibly a lump sum payment. I was entirely ignorant of the details, so I immediately telephoned the Royal College of Nursing, of which Mary was a member, to ask for their help and advice. This call, and my subsequent covering letter sent to the R.C.N. setting out all the details that I knew of Mary's nursing career, were the first of many that I made and wrote during the coming year. In those early months I was hampered, because all the telephone calls had to be made from public boxes, so as to shield Mary from learning that the disease was Huntington's chorea.

From the start I asked the R.C.N. if they could recover the overtime pay owing to Mary for the period April to October 1978. The Hilton Area Health Authority paid the August to October months, but they said that they could not find Mary's overtime claim slip for July. Payment for the April to July period was never made.

The loss of the July slip was only one of a number of administrative errors made by the H.A.H.A.. As early as December they had written to me, claiming that they had not received any certificates for Mary. I had sent the certificates off to them and Mary had received social security payments, which proved that the certificates had been posted on but not recorded by them.

More complications arose when Dr. Field, unsolicited and unauthorised, wrote to the H.A.H.A. asking for Mary to be pensioned off. They somewhat naively interpreted this to mean that Mary wished to retire forthwith. Had she gone straight on to pension she would not have received the greater financial benefit of six months at full and six months at half pay. It was

42

not until a senior nursing officer began to take personal responsibility for Mary's case soon afterwards, that the various difficulties resulting from inefficiency and Field's interference, were removed.

Dr. Clement, ever careful to observe my wish that Mary should not learn the full truth, continued to write 'involuntary movements' on her medical certificates. With Field's revelation to the Area Health Authority that Mary had Huntington's chorea, I feared that one of the administrative assistants would carelessly reveal the fact to her. Therefore, I rushed at the earliest opportunity to Dr. Clement, to ask if he would instruct the H.A.H.A. to show care in any communications. Dr. Clement was obliged to write to them, emphasizing that he did not wish Mary to learn that she had Huntington's chorea, or to be subjected to any unnecessary stress.

At a later date, the Department for Health and Social Security, apparently dissatisfied with Field's diagnosis, demanded an independent medical examination of Mary, before they would continue to pay Invalidity Benefit. Dr. Clement had to write and tell them that he did not want any interference with, or any pressure upon, Mary.

These are examples of the practical problems and difficulties that I faced at the time. It is not a comprehensive account, but it is indicative of the unnecessary stress that people are subjected to by inefficiency and callous insensitivity, just when they are least able to cope with it.

* * *

Before the onset of the disease, out of choice, we had limited ourselves to seeing a film, or going to a concert, or visiting friends only one or two evenings each week. Usually we would stay at home to read or listen to the radio, or, most enjoyable of all, to sit outside beneath the stars listening to gramophone records through headphones. Those weekends when Mary was off duty, we often walked in the Chilterns or the North Downs, and in the summer months we would camp. Our interests were mutual and we shared them. It never occurred to either of us to exclude the other one from any leisure activity, and except when working, we were always together. Through the years of our marriage this was so natural to us, that it went unnoticed.

The year 1978 had been fractious and full of stress, but our life style had remained similar to the previous years. Following the diagnosis, which clarified our hopeless future, it changed dramatically, bringing to an end the moderate and conservative style in which we lived. No longer were we content to remain quietly at home, but instead, we started on a restless round of activities which took us out almost every day. Anxious as we were to fill every moment, and never to be faced with a blank weekend or evening, I would plan the weeks and even months ahead with meticulous care. We went to all the local theatrical productions, the local concerts, to every ballet or poetry-reading. We used no critical judgement in our choice; we had no choice. We were forced to devour omnivorously both the third rate and the meritorious, in order to leave few empty hours which might cause us to weaken in the face of our dreadful situation.

One involvement, starting at that time, was with the local Caledonian Society. It was through this society that Mary and I were introduced to Scottish country dancing, a most unlikely pursuit for someone suffering from Huntington's chorea. In the future, this activity was to be both fruitful and fateful.

Chapter 4

Shortly after Mary's diagnosis, I was told by a colleague that a five-minute programme dealing with Huntington's chorea had been shown on television. It had been produced by an organisation called, 'Fight Huntington's Chorea'. He had scribbled down details of Fight's name and address to give to me. I wrote off immediately to obtain literature from them, and they sent me several old newsletters, and a booklet, explaining the disease for lay people.

Fight was founded in 1971 by May Stone, a lady whose father had been destroyed by Huntington's chorea. She started it as a self-help group for victims and their families, and also to disseminate information about the disease. Throughout the past century governments, doctors, and afflicted families, either intentionally or by default, had caused the disease to be shrouded in a 'conspiracy of silence'. I have already dealt with my own experience of this continuing 'conspiracy'.

The Fight literature added a wealth of information about the disease to that which I already held, and successive newsletters through the following years kept me informed of new developments. Although I was keenly interested in this literature, it did induce more despair in me. It presented fresh and disturbing facets of the disease that were not touched upon in medical textbooks. I believed that it was advisable to be as fully informed as possible, in order to be equipped to cope with future problems, but there was a price to be paid for this knowledge. I learned, for example, that the symptoms of H.C. are protean, and although some are common to most victims, they vary in severity between individuals. I also learned that the speed of deterioration cannot be anticipated, so in trepidation, I daily watched and waited for new symptoms to appear in Mary.

I was careful to arrange with Fight for all letters to be sent to my office, so that Mary would not see them. I was told that similar arrangements were made by other recipients of their literature.

The role of Fight was not limited to disseminating information from their central office. There were local branches with social and fund-raising events, and their activities, too, were reported in the newsletters. But from the moment that I read the first batch of literature, I became aware of an omission that was at first puzzling, and in succeeding months aroused my anger. Whilst there were items explaining the scientific research that was being done in different parts of the world, not one line touched, even lightly, upon the simple, cheap, and most effective way to eliminate the disease. The society had the crusading title of 'Fight', but it was misleading, for nowhere was there any mention of the necessity for choreics, and people at risk to the disease, to stop procreating.

* * *

Shortly after receiving that first batch of literature from Fight, I made the only move that I was ever to make to enlist their help. I was worried that should I meet with a sudden accident, or develop an illness causing my death, Mary would immediately be placed in a vulnerable position. We had made simple wills in which all property would be inherited by the other in the event of the death of one of us, but the advent of the disease introduced complicating factors that I feared might make them inadequate. I was uncomfortably aware that Mary's father, who was an unscrupulous man, would become her next of kin in the event of my death. With the progression of the disease, Mary might become either open to pressure from him to control her material assets, that is, our house and savings, or he might by legal means assume control as her father and next of kin. Another possibility, which would not affect Mary, but which irked me, was that he might persuade Mary, in her enfeebled state, to alter her will and make him and his second wife, and Mary's young half-brother, sole beneficiaries, following her death. But, my primary concern was the frightening possibility, that in pursuit of material gain, he might hasten her commitment to hospital. I presumed that Mary's sister-in-law Judy would oppose any nefarious moves by him, but there was no guarantee that she would be effective.

Eight months later, when I was with my eldest niece, I asked her if my fears and suspicions were justified. She believed that they were, and that Mary's father was untrustworthy.

I reasoned that Fight, drawing from their experience of the many complex legal and social situations that derive from H.C., might be able to advise me. They had a 'Samaritan' line that was available one evening each week, and it was manned by a social worker.

I telephoned Mrs Jenkins from a call box and put my inquiry, but she was not able to give me an immediate answer. It was agreed that I would ring one week later, and meantime she would make her own inquiries regarding the legal status of a person suffering from Huntington's chorea. When I telephoned her a second time, she informed me that she was unable to provide any information. Perhaps, I thought, she had been advised not to make comments to me about such a specialised legal field.

That second call was most memorable for the conversation that then followed. I considered that it was necessary, even my duty, to inform Mrs Jenkins about my recent experiences of the 'conspiracy of silence' that surrounded the disease. In those early months I was rather naïve, and I believed that she might take up the matter with the people concerned. I explained all the circumstances of Jim's and Mary's diagnoses, naming the different doctors. My brief narrative was delivered with indignation and anger, but to my surprise, apart from asking me to repeat Field's name, her only reaction was to say, "Oh".

I was rapidly learning that 'Fight' was a misnomer. Mrs Jenkins was neither surprised nor concerned by my story. It was obvious that she did not consider that she bore any moral responsibility for eliminating the disease. But, it was a disease that nightly made me wish death would take me, and every morning, on my awakening, regret that it had not done so, as consciousness returned me to fear and despair. Sensing that she was not reaching me, she finally suggested that I might find solace by going to church!

A week later I went to my solicitor to discuss with him the possibility of Mary's disinheritance in the future. I anticipated that I would have difficulty in making him understand the uncertainties attached to Huntington's chorea, because it does not lend itself to a firm prognosis. Fortunately, it was a mistaken assumption. He quickly grasped the problems, but his attitude, influenced, no doubt, by professional experience of human greed, betrayed suspicion of my own motive in consulting with him. It was frustrating to be misunderstood, but if I were correct in my belief, it was comforting that he was suspicious of me in his concern for Mary's interests. It gave me confidence that he would protect her as well as he was able to, in the event of my death.

Without hesitation, he thought of a suitable solution to the problem, and informed me that the best way to ensure that Mary could never be placed at the mercy of her father, would be to transfer ownership of our house solely to me, and to set up a trust, consisting of two or three reliable people, to administer it for Mary, should I predecease her.

I discussed this advice with a few friends in the weeks that followed, but Mary firmly opposed the proposal. She was distressed by the suggestion that she would be unable to live independently in the future. Perhaps my judgement was bad to remind her of this, for it was unlikely that her father would outlive me. Nevertheless, until her father died two years later, this possibility continued to worry me.

* * *

Early in 1979, I was advised by friends that a television programme about Huntington's chorea, produced by Fight, was to be shown in the following week. I telephoned other friends to suggest that they view it. I was surprised when two of them, and also my brother, told me that they had seen the programme advertised in the Radio Times and decided that it would be inadvisable for me to watch it. They considered that it might give me unnecessary stress, so they had not forewarned me. This patronising opinion was demeaning, and revealed how little they understood me.

Mary and I did not have a television set, so on the pretext of walking the dog, I left the house to see the programme with friends living nearby. It lasted for thirty minutes. It dealt with the disease in general terms, and in addition, it filmed and interviewed a family in which the mother was afflicted. There were notable omissions which made the programme less than honest. The filming of an advanced patient with the disease was very brief, and during the closing minutes, when a plea was made for victims to be treated as humanely as possible when they are finally admitted to hospital, actors passively seated in wheelchairs to represent patients, were used. Had real patients been used, and their symptoms explained to viewers, most reasonable people would have concluded that lavishing care upon advanced sufferers could not be sufficient to make their lives worthwhile. I remembered Mary's severely disabled patient, and contrasted her condition with this emasculated representation of the disease.

The programme, then, was altogether too bland. There was not one contributor who spoke with passion of the suffering and the destruction of human relationships that the disease brings. This made Huntington's chorea even less noteworthy for the general viewer.

It was when the programme dealt with the afflicted family, that the moral abdication of Fight was clearly revealed. They were a family of six: mother, father, and four adult children. The mother's decline had started five years earlier. She explained that she had never been told that she was at risk to Huntington's chorea. The disease had come as a total surprise. She talked about some of her day-to-day difficulties. She mentioned that she was deprived of the pleasure that walking had once given her, because she was unable to go far now. She had difficulty with numbers, and when laying a table, for example, she was unable to count the correct number of places that were needed. Her facial chorea was pronounced, and her slurred speech would soon become arcane.

Although she was in a relatively early stage of Huntington's chorea, the symptoms that she mentioned were distressing, and I could infer like everyone else involved with the disease who was watching, the likely emotional problems of the family that were not mentioned.

The father, and a son and daughter were interviewed. The father spoke sadly about his fears for the children; each one was at a one in two chance of having inherited the disease. Following him, his son, who was soon to be married, mentioned his decision not to have children. Finally, the daughter came on. She was already married, and to my horror and rage calmly announced that she was taking the risk of having children, and was already seven months pregnant!

Not a word of criticism, or the slightest doubt was expressed, in the programme commentary following the daughter's statement. Clearly and unambiguously, by the absence of even the mildest reproof, Fight revealed itself to be not merely irresponsible but dangerous, because it condoned the transmission of the disease.

* * *

I was to hear this expression 'taking the risk' on a number of occasions in the future. The man or woman at risk to Huntington's chorea, who knowingly and deliberately has children does not take any risk. Their own fate has been sealed at the moment of their conception. Either they have inherited the fatal gene or they have not. No action of theirs can in any way influence this fate. It is their innocent children who have to bear the risk, and who, being unborn, have no choice.

Consider the position of people who are at risk. It is truly terrible. They may have a grandparent with the disease, or one who has died as a result of it. Their own parent may for the moment be unaffected, but until that parent reaches old age without the disease breaking out, they cannot relax in the secure knowledge that they will not inherit it. They will, by this time, be middle-aged. For half their lives they will have lived under the constant threat of the disease breaking out. Daily they may observe themselves for the slightest tremor, or the first signs of poor balance, or a lapse of memory, or an uncharacteristic hesitation as they speak, or write, or add together a column of figures. They may have deliberately refrained from marriage, being unwilling to impose their potentially premature destruction upon another person. They may have married but behaved honourably, by carefully avoiding begetting children. They may have denied themselves entry into certain professions or entrepreneurial business, fearful of the consequences should they break out with the disease.

Terrible though the position may be for those who live through the first half of their lives at risk to the disease, consider the fate of those people who have a parent at risk, who dies prematurely, that is, before reaching old age, or a parent who actually has the disease. They are condemned, even should they not have inherited the fatal gene, to a lifetime of the experience of being at risk to the disease. For them, there is left only the faint hope that scientific research may lead to a cure. Their lives are effectively ruined.

* * *

Parliamentary legislation will be needed to enable the health authorities to commit into custody all those suffering from, and at risk to, the disease until they agree to be sterilised, that is, until they are no longer dangerous to society. Meanwhile it is vital that people involved with affected families should attempt to understand the reasons for the remarkable fact that, in spite of being fully informed about the disease, many continue to breed.

Friends, doctors, and social workers, should make it their paramount aim to persuade members of afflicted families not to have children. This policy should take precedence over any other considerations.

It is probable that affected families have their share of feckless members who give no thought to the future. But, it is my belief that many people are motivated to have children by powerful forces, which come directly from the fearful position of having the disease, or being at risk to it. It must be extremely difficult for them to make the unpalatable admission that their birth was not an accident. Perhaps their parents produced them in spite of knowing that there was a serious hereditary disorder in the family, or because they did not bother to inquire closely into the reason why relatives ended mysteriously in mental hospitals. If they have a loving, or merely an affectionate relationship with parents, the revelation to a teenager or a young adult, that their parents have knowingly put them at risk to the disease, must be stupefying. I cannot comprehend it, but I am certain that it is explosive to learn that your parents, those to whom you so often return for succour, have utterly betrayed you. It must be easier to pretend that having children, whilst at risk to H.C., or suffering from it, is normal and natural.

It must be at least as explosive, and in my opinion even more difficult, to integrate the knowledge that society, in general, has failed to stop your birth. It may be possible for some people to ignore the moral inadequacy of only two people who happen to be their parents. It is far more difficult to ignore the society in which you live, in which large numbers of people, including successive Ministers for Health, doctors and social workers, have taken no action, and continue to take no action, to trace all affected and at-risk people, to stop them breeding. Faced with this terrible and continuing indifference, which contrasts so markedly with a Western society's traditional concern for the individual's moral and material needs, how easy it must be for affected and at-risk individuals to enter the illusion that H.C. is a normal part of life. From this evasion, it is rational to go on to have your own children just like everyone else!

In addition to these reasons causing people from affected families to procreate, it is unlikely that anyone at risk would be allowed to adopt children to satisfy their parental desires. Adoption agencies cannot take the chance of passing on children to couples where one partner may break out with Huntington's chorea, irrevocably ruining a childhood, and perhaps, in consequence, harming an adult life. They will always choose, in preference, couples who are healthy and likely to remain so. This anomaly, that people actually with the disease, or at risk to it, are permitted to breed freely, but are unlikely to be allowed to adopt, is another example of the double standards that society has towards Huntington's chorea.

There is one final observation that I must make in answer to those bigots who believe in the right of people to procreate, whatever the consequences. There are many people who deny themselves the pleasures of parenthood because their spouse is at risk to the disease. These people show laudable concern for the unborn. It is very unfair that they feel obliged to deprive themselves because of the feckless behaviour of the at-risk parents, who did choose to procreate. The sacrifices made by these responsible people will have to continue, until affected families stop breeding.

* * *

It steadily emerged through those early months that Fight chose to avoid any criticism of choreics or people at risk, who were continuing to have children. Fight's officers and members were not morally neutral in their policies. They did help affected people, those at risk to the disease, and people caring for the sick, and they supported research into a cure for the disease. But, they did not promote any move to eradicate the disease in the only practical manner currently available, that is, to isolate in custody all affected families until they agreed to be sterilised. I have been told by one of Fight's officers, that all topics are discussed at their meetings except for sterilisation. Fight, then, cares only for its membership of afflicted families, and it is indifferent towards the unborn.

Fight's unstated but clear moral abdication was far more damaging than it at first appeared to be. References to Huntington's chorea on the radio, by medical authors, by doctors and social workers, or, at a later date, by my Member of Parliament and the Minister for Health when I corresponded with them, invariably included mention of Fight. They all recommended it as the body that affected people should turn to for support. Thus, the existence of Fight enabled them to avoid any personal responsibility or commitment towards eliminating the disease.

Members of Parliament in particular, can safely avoid taking any stance on the issues involved, whilst Fight, recognized to be the national society concerned with the disease, remains silent. Were Fight a militant pressure group, stridently calling for action to protect the unborn, they might have to respond with suitable legislation.

I did consider attending Fight meetings with the aim of recruiting sympathetic people to form a pressure group, and I was urged to do so by a friend, who believed that it was essential for someone to lift the society out of its inertia. But, she did not understand the violence of the emotions that these people would probably arouse in me. Whilst being fully informed about the disease, many of them were responsible for transmitting it or condoning its transmission. If I attended a meeting, it would have been solely for the purpose of raising the question of sterilisation. The certain hostility that this would have drawn, might have produced a very angry reaction from me. I dared not go near them.

* * *

It was inevitable that Mary would learn at some time that the disease she had inherited was Huntington's chorea, but I had asked people not to disclose it to her. In some cases I had written, and one letter had been sent to my sister-in-law, Judy. I had specifically asked her not to allow Jim to speak by telephone to Mary. By then Jim never telephoned independently; either he lacked the initiative, or he was unable to dial the numbers.

I made this request, because shortly before the diagnosis, Mary's father had made what was to be his final visit to our house during a short holiday with Jim and Judy. I had been out, but Mary told me afterwards, that in referring to Jim's symptoms he had remarked that Jim looked just like his mother. Shortly after this visit, Jim, when talking to Mary, had maliciously insisted that their father had referred to her, not to him. I feared that out of a wish to hurt Mary he would not hesitate to tell her that it was H.C., once he knew. For him, the revelation of the name of his condition would not be very significant, unpleasant and fearful though the memory of his mother might be. For Mary, knowledge that it was Huntington's chorea would be devastating.

It was. I returned home one day to find Mary looking pale and shaken, far in excess of her usual anxious state. Judy had talked with her by telephone, and then handed the receiver to Jim. Just as I had anticipated, he had immediately told Mary that she had Huntington's chorea. I admitted to her that I had known for several months. It was a slight and temporary relief for me that she now knew the truth, and that she could better understand my own reactions to our situation. But, this was trivial when contrasted with her new knowledge, that she could hardly have received a worse inheritance from her mother.

* * *

In July 1979, just a few months after this telephone conversation with her brother, Mary was subjected to further distressing revelations about her condition. This time it was accidental. I read in the Radio Times about a series of Radio 4 programmes called 'Lifelines in Medicine', and one of them dealt with Parkinson's disease and Huntington's chorea. On the evening of the broadcast, I sat outside to hear it using headphones, so that Mary would believe I was listening to music.

The programme started with Parkinson's disease. It was interesting; an unpleasant ailment, but not memorable, and it was soon disposed of. It was followed by a discussion on Huntington's chorea that was very different from the television programme produced by Fight. It was factual, and uncompromising in its presentation of material. The programme touched upon the great suffering within afflicted families because of the lengthy period between onset and death, and of the high suicide rate attributable to the disease, which was an indication of suffering. The question of sterilising choreics and people at risk was introduced, with the point being made that by taking this measure the disease could be eliminated. As quickly as it had been introduced the subject was dropped. Neither of the two speakers was in favour of sterilisation, presumably preferring the 'great suffering' to continue, but then neither of them were closely involved with the disease and experiencing the suffering.

Towards the end of the programme a twenty-nine year old woman suffering from the disease was interviewed. Her speech was slurred, and it sounded weird as though her mouth was half full of food. Her early life had been ruined, because her father had been afflicted with H.C. throughout her childhood. He had made life miserable for the family with his extreme irritability and rapid changes of mood. She had always been frightened to return home from school, not knowing in what state of mind her father would be. When she was adolescent she had been told that her father had Huntington's chorea, and that she was at a one-in-two risk of inheriting it. Years later, when she had broken out with the disease, her employer, learning of this, had fired her. She ended by saying that she would never be able to marry and have children.

The programme was harrowing, and the hopeless future for victims, inevitably leading to their incarceration in mental hospitals, was clearly stated. When I went indoors, it was to find that Mary had chanced to turn on her portable radio and had heard the programme. She was shocked

56

and in tears. I did not know what to say to her. We were realists, and Mary, in particular, always rejected pretence. I believe it was from this time, that she fully accepted she could not afford to wait too long for the disease to erode her mind and disable her body. If she did, she ran the risk of losing the initiative, and the physical capability, that is required for a successful suicide.

Chapter 5

The reactions of other people to the calamity that had befallen us varied widely. From the beginning some friends evinced an inability to understand the prognosis of the disease. One of them did not know it was hereditary as late as one year after Mary's diagnosis, in spite of numerous references being made to it in our conversations during visits. This led me to the belief that they were too involved in their own lives to give more than cursory attention to us, beyond the confines of the common ground in which our friendships had developed. Most of them, although knowledgeable about the nature of the disease and the manner of its transmission, showed reluctance to agree with me, that it could easily be stopped from spreading by coercing affected families into sterilisation. I concluded from this, that they could hardly regard what was visibly happening to Mary with the concern, or even horror, that I expected from friends, if they did not consider it necessary to stop it happening to other people.

Some friends gradually withdrew from us. I presumed they knew that they lacked the qualities needed to respond in a helpful manner to our desperate situation. Possibly, too, they were frightened, or even embarrassed by us.

Others told me, possibly truthfully at first, but mendaciously as the disease progressed, that they could not see much wrong with Mary. Apart from ignoring the dreadful facts of the prognosis, this implied that the disease was not especially harmful to us or to our marriage. They seemed too superficial to appreciate how damaging Huntington's chorea is to a relationship, even in its early stages.

One friend advised me to see a social worker, or a psychiatrist, or to take prescribed drugs, in order to be able to cope. This implied that I was sick, either because of my angry expressions of moral outrage at what was happening to Mary, and the general indifference towards us, or because the erosion of my marriage had produced quite natural feelings of emotional deprivation. For either reason her advice was demeaning. She also held to the belief that I could manage for a decade or more, in what would be a steadily worsening situation. Her arbitrary, and utterly mistaken opinion on my ability to manage for such a long period, was enforced by her freely expressed belief that it was my duty to do so.

There were, of course, the inevitable invitations to 'Come round', or 'phone if ever you feel the need to talk about it'. Since I continually felt like unburdening myself, sometimes acutely, and at most inconvenient hours, I decided that to accept these invitations literally would quickly lead to their withdrawal. I also had to accept, that it was unlikely that these friends would be able to respond to the concomitant changes that Huntington's chorea had brought to Mary and me, and they would be unable, even if willing, to afford me any solace.

When I telephoned my brother soon after the diagnosis to tell him what was happening to Mary, I was surprised to learn that he knew something about the disease. He remembered with distress, an ex-Battle of Britain pilot, who had suffered from it many years ago, and from this he concluded that our situation could hardly be worse. But during another call when I spoke bitterly to him about the hereditary transmission, criticising the widespread irresponsibility that had led to Mary's birth, he reacted with hostility, telling me not to preach to him. It seemed that he felt his basic assumptions were being threatened by my definitive opinions on the need to control the disease.

Following this second telephone call, I remembered that when I had visited him whilst he was in a mental hospital a few years earlier, he was hardly enjoying the experience, and chafing to get out. He was able, at the time, to anticipate his discharge, but Mary, once she was admitted to hospital, would never leave. This telephone call marked yet another rejection. My brother was unwilling to accept my level of need, therefore,

I reciprocated by rejecting him. I never telephoned again.

Then there was the daughter of one of Mary's ex patients who called one day. Mary happened to be out, but she stopped to talk with me. Marilyn spoke with warm admiration for Mary's care of her mother, and expressed concern for her now that she had Huntington's chorea. We discussed the situation, and amongst other matters, I explained how we were going out nightly and why.

"No, no", this woman exclaimed, "That's not the way to live. You must trust in Jesus!"

Evidently she was a Christian, who believed that she had the answer to our problems. Unfortunately, she did not explain how to trust in Jesus, or how this would stop the atrophy of Mary's brain. In an attempt, apparently to be helpful, she went on to tell me about her brother, whose wife had developed cancer and died three years later. Glowingly, she described how, following his wife's death, he had married a beautiful young girl, who had borne him two children.

I presumed that this piece of biography was to encourage me to take a more optimistic view of my future. Possibly, it may have eased any fears that she felt about the capricious disasters that characterise life. She conveniently chose to overlook that the average life-span of people afflicted with H.C. is fifteen years, not three. Shortly afterwards she invited Mary to lunch, but other than a chance meeting two years later, Mary heard nothing more of her.

A year later I was to have a very similar experience with friends who lived near to us. We had arranged to visit them, but following yet another bitter crisis Mary refused to go, so I went alone. In Mary's absence the situation was discussed, and I touched upon my own fear of the future. Neal then talked about one of his colleagues whose wife had died of cancer. This man, he explained, had at first been shaken, but within a year he had recovered from the loss. I would, too, Neal assured me.

Like Marilyn, Neal was dishonest in failing to make any distinction between a man whose wife dies following a short illness, and myself, with a wife who would deteriorate over many years in a particularly unpleasant manner.

In the months following Mary's diagnosis, I sometimes telephoned friends from the privacy of public boxes. This practice came to an abrupt end one evening, following a call to ask Jane for advice. She peremptorily said that I would have to make my own decisions. I declared that I could not, and that it was unfair that the calamity had been imposed upon me. She tartly rejoindered that I was imposing upon her. I rang off immediately.

With one notable exception a year later, I never again telephoned friends to ask for help or advice, no matter how desperate I felt. Following that rebuff, we never visited anyone without a firm invitation. We rarely invited people to our home, so that those who did come were usually uninvited. In our unhappy state, we had lost the balance and poise that enables people to give and receive in harmonious friendships. Three years later, I had lost all but one of the friendships made in the period of my life before the inception of the disease. This, too, is an example of the destructive effect of Huntington's chorea.

* * *

During a consultation with my doctor for a trivial ailment, I talked to him about Mary and her despair. He responded by saying that he would like a local health visitor to call on Mary. He added that she was a very kind person. I had never made any requests to him, other than those that I have mentioned above concerning Mary's employer and the Social Security office. I was doubtful about this proposed visit. I could not see Mary being beguiled away from her despair, and it might give her additional pain to be treated openly as a sick person dependent upon a

Health Service worker.

Mrs Cattell was as kind as Dr Clement had claimed her to be. She visited Mary just once, and in confidence afterwards, she admitted to me that she had found it difficult, in view of Mary's hopeless future, to say anything constructive to her. Mary confirmed Mrs Cattell's impotence when commenting to me later about the visit, saying, "What can Mrs Cattell do for me?'" Obviously, it was humiliating for Mary to endure the pretence that she was receiving help when none was available.

In isolation, this visit was not of great significance, but it did lead to a painful experience for us at a later date, because Mrs Cattell followed it by arranging an introduction to a social worker. Mrs Cattell explained that the social worker would ensure that Mary received all the allowances that might be due to her.

The four of us met at the local health visitors' office. Mrs King was probably in her fifties. She was chatty, cheerful, and very extroverted. She said that other than the Invalidity Benefit that Mary was already receiving, there was nothing more that we were entitled to claim. To my surprise, Mrs King, gushing on said that, at a later date, we would be entitled to an orange 'disabled' disc in the car. At the time I believed that this cruelly tactless remark in Mary's presence was a faux-pas, but at our next meeting with her I was disabused of this tolerant opinion.

By chance, I met Mrs Cattell a few weeks later. It was shortly after the showing of Fight's programme on television. She had seen it, and was critically surprised that there are people who withhold information from those who are at risk, and people like the daughter who entered into parenthood. It was Mrs Cattell who first coined for me the phrase 'conspiracy of silence', that so aptly described one of the principal reasons why we still have the disease in Britain. It may seem unimportant that one health visitor should express intelligent humanism, but I found her reaction to the programme reassuring. It made me feel less isolated.

Several months passed before Mrs King entered our lives again. She telephoned one day saying that she wished to have a second meeting with us, this time at our home. She wished to place Mary on the disabled register. I agreed to the former request, but demurred at the latter. I said that putting Mary on the register could only cause her more distress, and I asked what purpose it would serve. Mrs King did not answer this question, she merely repeated that she would like Mary to go on to it. I agreed upon condition that Mary was not told.

Mrs King duly came, but her visit was memorably painful. I had asked her not to call, as I could not see what purpose she could serve, but I did not wish to make a pre-judgement. We started with general conversation, but soon this changed when I spoke bitterly about the irresponsibility which had brought this catastrophe upon us. Unlike Mrs Cattell, she did not respond favourably to my intensely expressed sense of injustice. She apparently lacked any decent moral judgement on the issues involved, and therefore could not possibly be of any assistance to us beyond giving advice on purely material matters. It was impossible for me to accept help from any person whose opinions were those which lead to the continuing transmission of the disease, and in our case had led to Mary's birth. One does not accept alms from the hand of the person who has put one into beggary.

Mrs King was even more stupid and ignorant than I had reason to suspect from the first meeting. She professed with pride to have some knowledge of Huntington's chorea, adding that she had attended meetings where the disease had been discussed. But, she mistakenly believed that all afflicted people had little intellectual comprehension, implying that from the moment of the inception of the disease, victims became cretinous. As if to prove the sincerity of her outrageous and misinformed belief, she then said in the presence of Mary, that at a later date we would be eligible for a grant for handrails to be fitted in the bathroom. Then, apparently wishing to placate my strongly expressed sense of helpless frustration, she suggested, still in the presence of Mary, that brain tissue could be donated for research. Most unforgiveable, because it could not be excused on the grounds of her fatuous beliefs, she produced a form that required Mary's own signature in order to be placed on the disabled register. Mrs King had deliberately lied to me when promising that Mary would not be told.

Following this meeting, I drafted a letter to the Social Services in which I briefly set out why I did not wish to see Mrs King again. I asked them for the name of another social worker whom I could contact, should I need one in the future. I showed this draft to local health visitors and asked for their opinions.

They advised me not to send it. They warned me that I might make difficulties for myself in the future. They advised me to make a request, that if I needed the assistance of a social worker, I wished this to be arranged through my health visitor, not direct with the Social Services office. This arrangement, they explained, would stop any more unwanted visits from social workers. I followed their advice and sent a suitable letter.

In retrospect, I was concerned at the pain this woman probably gave to sick and disabled people who had to bear her gross personal and professional inadequacies. Earlier in that year one of my friends had shrewdly warned me against any involvement with social workers. He considered that they would have to be unusual people if they were to be of any help to us. But, even he would not have expected anyone quite like Mrs King.

* * *

In that summer of 1979, Dr. Clement retired. In view of Mary's health, which made it necessary for our doctor to be a person sympathetically aware of our problems, I was apprehensive whilst waiting for the arrival of his successor, Dr. Parikh. We did not have to wait long before we saw him, because shortly after his arrival we received a form from Mary's employer which required his signature. It was almost a year since Mary had stopped working. For the first six months she had received full pay, and in the following months it had been reduced to half-pay. After one year all pay would cease, and she would receive a lump sum payment and a monthly pension from the National Health Service scheme to which she had contributed. Dr Parikh was required by the Hilton Area Health Authority to complete this form, confirming that Mary had Huntington's chorea, and was therefore unable to work and eligible for a pension.

We made an appointment, and on the day entered his surgery together. I handed him the form and explained the requirement. Dr Parikh took out Mary's wallet and began leafing through, carefully reading each document. We sat watching silently, and as usual when Mary was faced with discussion of her condition, she became pale and frightened. It was quite obvious that he had not bothered to check Mary's medical background. In his position, in a new practice, and not knowing anything about his patients, he should have been careful to acquaint himself with background information before the consultation.

Finally, he looked up, turned to Mary, and asked what her symptoms were. Not expecting this she was silent, frightened and staring. I protested immediately, that we were in a catastrophic situation, that he had the neurologist's report, and surely that was sufficient.

He replied that he had to enter something, and turning back to Mary asked her curtly if she experienced shaking.

"Yes", I said, "write that down".

It appeared that he knew nothing about the disease, it hardly exists in the Sub-Continent. Only the word 'chorea' seemed to mean anything to him.

Following this consultation, it was clear to me that in view of Dr. Parikh's ignorance of the disease, we would have to change to another doctor. This proved to be difficult, because local doctors had full complements of patients. We were turned away by several, in spite of Mary's previous contact with them as a district nurse. Eventually, Mary did find one who would take us. Dr. Hender was kind and well informed about Huntington's chorea, and she had worked with him in the past, but his surgery was almost two miles away. Mary was not allowed to drive, and in the future, as the disease progressed, she would become less mobile, so it was advisable to find someone who was nearer. Finally, a local doctor whose surgery was one mile away agreed to accept us. I would have preferred someone close, but we had no other option.

* * *

Nine months after the diagnosis, we were in the mid-summer of 1979. The fine weather brought us no pleasure. Normally we would go walking in the Chilterns at every opportunity, or we would sit in our garden during the warm evenings. For these pleasures we had substituted a restless round of theatre and cinema going, and thrown ourselves into the social activities of the local Caledonian Society. I could not bear to be alone with Mary, so our previous close relationship had become a serious disadvantage. We had not developed our lives separately through the past twenty years, and this fact had been extolled by our friends, if ever they commented on our marriage.

By now, Mary was becoming more isolated. Only one friend visited her regularly, and some not at all. Several could have called whilst I was at work should they have preferred to see Mary alone. She needed people to talk with, for the disruption of our relationship inhibited her when she was with me. She did have occasional visits from nursing colleagues early in 1979, but these had stopped. Somewhat tactlessly, the Supervisor of Nurses confided to me a year later, that she had instigated these. It appeared that out of obligation and feelings of guilt for neglecting Mary, she sought to exonerate herself in this manner. I never told Mary that the visits had not been spontaneous, but for me it made them morally dubious.

In addition to the loss of contact with friends and severance from her work, she continued to be the recipient of my freely expressed anger and frustration. At a later date, a neighbour suggested that perhaps Mary was fortified by what she may have seen as my strength of personality, that is, my refusal to compromise on the moral issues surrounding Huntington's chorea.

In that first year following diagnosis, I did have a firm commitment to Mary, which ensured the continuation of my sense of outrage with the society that had allowed her to inherit the disease. Had I not been committed to her care and protection, the consequent indifference to her fate would have greatly reduced my bitter anger. She paid a high price for this commitment because of the frequent furores which were set off by my inability to suffer in silence.

Occasionally, she would escape to her brother and sister-in-law, for temporary refuge from the more violent of my tirades against the people who had been responsible for bringing the disease to us. Once, early in 1979, she had fled to find that her brother, Jim, was alone. She had found him distressing to observe, knowing that she was destined to deteriorate to his pitiful condition. She had used the visit to question him closely about his symptoms and problems. She wanted to learn from his experience, so that she would be able to understand the difficulties that might arise for us in the future. She was anxious to please me and to salvage our faltering marriage.

* * *

Mary was, as I have written above, realistic, and often a little cynical about life. Add to this her vast experience of the degrading and painful nature of some terminal illnesses that she had witnessed through many years of district nursing, and it was not surprising to me, that, from the day she was diagnosed, she began to think and talk about suicide.

Quite early in 1979 I had introduced the subject to Dr Clement, but he would not be drawn. Whatever his opinion about Mary's future, the 1961 Suicide Act may have been sufficient to deter him from discussing it with me. Later that year, when I mentioned Mary's growing conviction that ultimately she must kill herself, a neighbour suggested we contact the Euthanasia Society. This almost casual reference was to lead to events in our lives that I would have dismissed as implausible, had they been used in a work of fiction.

I was vaguely aware of the existence of the society. In a country like Britain, with a tradition of radical movements covering every lost cause that people with liberal consciences support, it was inevitable that there would be one. The Euthanasia Society was founded in 1935, making it the oldest of its type in the world. Its object was to change the law through parliamentary legislation, so that with adequate legal safeguards, people suffering from incurable, painful, or degrading diseases, could, if they wished, receive assistance to die painlessly.

With the passing of the 1961 Act it was no longer an offence to attempt suicide, but it remained an offence punishable by up to fourteen years imprisonment, to aid, abet, counsel, or procure a suicide. The Act removed the antiquated Judeo-Christian-derived anomaly that had made a suicide attempt a criminal offence, but it substituted legislation that was patently irrational and unfair in its enforcement.

For the individual, access to suicide is rather like a lottery, and dependent upon one's circumstances. It is blatantly discriminatory against those people who are confined to bed or housebound, and therefore unable to affect their own release from intolerable suffering. Theoretically, their suicide is perfectly legal, but for the person disabled by a severe stroke, or with advanced multiple sclerosis, for example, it is impossible in practice. These people have to rely upon the illegal assistance of their doctor, or family, or friends for release, and they may not get this. Even for those would-be suicides who are mobile, there is little or no information available on effective methods, and there is limited access to drugs. By contrast, doctors have both access and information.

In a humane society, suicide by the sick would disappear. Either individuals would be given support, so that in spite of having incurable diseases they would choose to continue living, or society would give euthanasia to those people who find their incurable diseases intolerable, and who ask for release from them. At present society does neither.

In 1976, National Opinion Poll Market Research Ltd. carried out a United Kingdom wide poll asking, 'Should the law allow adults to receive medical help to an immediate peaceful death, if suffering from incurable physical illness that is intolerable to them.........?' 69% approved, 17% disapproved, and 14% didn't know.

Following the Radio 4 programme on Huntington's chorea, Mary asked me to telephone The Euthanasia Society. I spoke to the General Secretary, Leslie Ford, outlining Mary's situation and mentioning her decision, in principle, to take her own life before her deterioration had progressed too far. He was sympathetic, and firmly agreed that Huntington's chorea was so terrible that it warranted suicide. He had listened to the Radio 4 programme the night before. He promised to send me literature on the Society and to include copies of their 'Advanced Declaration' form.

This form was the only practical help that the Society could give. Amongst other paragraphs it read, 'If there is no prospect of my recovery from physical illness or impairment expected to cause me severe distress or render me incapable of rational existence, I request that I be allowed to die and not be kept alive by artificial means and that I receive whatever quantity of drugs may be required to keep me free from pain or distress even if the moment of death is hastened'. A copy had to be signed and witnessed, and deposited with one's doctor. It was a passable legal safeguard against being treated contrary to a patient's wishes.

On receiving the literature we both joined the Society, and deposited signed and witnessed 'Advance Declaration' forms with our doctor. This latter move, which seemed at the time to be of little more note than taking out an insurance policy, was to be vitally important at a later date.

I also wrote to the Society in August expressing support. I explained that our latent belief in the need for voluntary euthanasia had been firmly crystallized now that Mary suffered with Huntington's chorea. I added that we were in favour of the proposed publication by the Society of a booklet, which would give practical information on methods of how to end one's life, painlessly.

From that moment, Mary started to cling to the hope that, with the proposed booklet beside her, she would have the means of release from her plight when she chose to use it. She knew that it was essential to retain control of her future. She had no intention of allowing the disease to take its course, which would lead to her committal to a mental institution, where like her mother, she might linger for many years. She might even suffer a fate similar to the patient with the disease she had nursed, who was not only helpless in a degrading physical and mental condition, but suffering the severe and constant pain of pressure sores.

In a situation from which there could be no escape for Mary and no happy ending, the prospect which most worried me, was also that of her incarceration in an institution, lonely and frightened. If I should meet with a fatal accident or disease, she might be forgotten and defenceless.

I was incapable of comprehending how Mary must have felt at that time. She remained stoical and silent, rarely mentioning her fears. To the outside world she often presented a cheerful front. In private she frequently looked frightened and hunted. She was faced with the awesome knowledge that, at some time in the future she must kill herself.

She must do this alone and unaided, with the possibility that it might be bungled, or that people might intervene and revive her, if I should not be on hand to stop them. She frequently said that "The only question is, when I should do it". She did not have the spur of physical pain to stiffen her resolution. If that ever came, as it had for her patient, she would be far beyond any possibility of effecting her own release.

* * *

With the approach of the August Bank Holiday, one of Mary's nieces telephoned to say that she and her two sisters would be at the family home over the weekend, and invited us to visit them. The remainder of the family would be away, she added. If I did not wish to see them, they were prepared to collect Mary by car. We accepted, and agreed to go on Friday.

We had not seen Barbara and Angela since their father was diagnosed. I felt a little nervous as we entered the house. I would have preferred not to be there. Our own situation was enough for us to bear. We did not know the extent of the sorrow or despair that we would find now that all four siblings were at a one-in-two risk of inheriting the disease. I also feared that they would show acceptance of the social irresponsibility that had placed them in such a frightful position. I knew that in any discussion I would be uncompromising in my stand, and then there would be friction.

There was a slow, somewhat cautious start to the conversation. The momentous events of the past year had radically altered our relationships, and we all displayed the sort of reserve normally shown to strangers, as we sought to establish new communicative lines. Soon we became more frank, and then, hardly conscious of myself, I launched into a diatribe against the society and the individuals who had wronged us. I covered all the ground, apportioning blame as I spoke. Just as I had feared, it turned into an abrasive encounter as Barbara and Catrina sought to reject my analysis. The exchange became even more heated when I was told that their brother Roy had become religious in reaction to his plight, and that he intended to have children when he married. He claimed that Jesus would see that he did not inherit H.C., but that even if he and his children did, it would not matter, because they would all be in His hands. The girls excitedly asserted his right to choose to have children, whilst I angrily condemned his evasion of responsibility.

It was plain that Catrina and Barbara were unable to accept that their at-risk position, their very birth, could and should have been avoided. They probably found it intolerable to acknowledge that their awesome situation was not accidental. It was not until Angela interceded quietly to agree with me, that we all became silent.

Following that contentious start, our visit became more rewarding. I really knew very little about my nieces. In part this was due to a generation gap that in its facile elements created an artificial barrier between us. I was frank about my own problems, and I believe that this led them to accept me because of the vulnerable humanity that it revealed.

We talked until 2.00 a.m.. Angela and Barbara told us that their visits home were infrequent, and that they lasted at most for two days. They could not bear to stay any longer in such a painful situation that presaged their own fearfully uncertain future. They both knew that they could never have children, and they told us that they had decided, in principle, upon suicide, should the disease be triggered off in them.

Angela agreed with me that the disease first became manifest in her father during 1970. She revealed, that whilst working in psychiatric hospitals she had seen patients with H.C., and suspected for years that it was this that afflicted her father. She had remained silent, not wishing to cause any unnecessary worry to anyone. She said that Jim had once broached the question of suicide to her, asking for information. She could not bring herself to offer any.

Angela came along to visit us two days later, and once again we talked for many hours. We discussed our problems at some depth, Angela attempting to bring comfort to Mary, but after she had left us the pleasure of her company was replaced by feelings of lonely desolation. Sharing our problems in discussion could not solve them. They were insuperable.

Chapter 6

At that time, Mary's deterioration seemed to proceed a little faster. Although it was never rapid, it did accelerate occasionally. I would observe her during these periods with fear and fascination, wondering if, or when, her decline would stop. It was rather like watching a descending lift that may have gone out of control.

The chorea, the erratic tripping gait, that is so characteristic of the disease, the rolling movements of her head, and her poor balance, had increased during the past year and were now very marked. She was even more forgetful, and less able to organise her life. Her reading was slower, and writing gave her more trouble, requiring intense effort. When we were searching for a new doctor I drafted a simple letter for her to send. She made four laborious attempts to copy this draft, spending several hours on them, before finally producing a satisfactory letter.

In addition, other symptoms had appeared. She lacked all finesse in her movements, and when she became hasty, due to nervousness, this magnified her clumsiness. Her speech had become noticeably less distinct. It was not only slightly slurred, but it had also begun to sound as if she had been given a local anaesthetic. Frequently, I had to ask her to repeat sentences. Her facial expression was increasingly vacuous, interspersed with attempts to concentrate, when she would knit her brow and take on a slightly puzzled expression about the eyes.

All these symptoms either increased as time passed or they remained static, with one notable exception, and this was the chorea. After 1979 it lessened, and apart from excessive pouting of her lips she was never troubled greatly by it, nor was it very obvious to an observer.

I met her one day in the High Street, and she staggered up to me with a loving smile, but I was sickened by despair at the travesty of her face, with its vacant expression and rolling eyes. I averted mine but there was no escape, for my downward look fastened upon her ankles, and I felt more black despair in noticing, for the first time, that her tights had myriad holes around the ankles, where her heels had caught them as she walked.

On another occasion when I unexpectedly saw her in the High St., she appeared at my first glance to be a familiar stranger. For a brief moment I saw her dispassionately, a weird disjointed figure standing out from the flow of the other pedestrians, like a drunk. And then with surprise and a weak sinking feeling I recognized her, and she became my responsibility. We were on opposite sides of the street and she had not seen me. I did not cross over; I passed by on the other side.

Cut off from her work, she spent considerable time doing housework. She tended to repeat herself, dusting the same ledges, for example, on consecutive days. As the months and years passed the proportion of time that she used to clean and re-clean increased. In part this was to fill in each lonely day, and in part because the disease and her depressed state made her slower. She also kept the house clean to please me. In later years, I would often rush home anxious to know that nothing untoward had happened to her in my absence. I might arrive in the middle of one of her interminable cleaning sessions, to find furniture and ornaments in most rooms of the house in disarray. In my state of chronic stress and irritation, and aware that it would be hours before everything would go back into its customary order, I would explode with anger. I had always preferred to live in an orderly manner, and throughout our marriage we had done so, but now I needed to do so in response to the chaos and uncertainty that the disease had brought to me. It seemed that I was constantly struggling to stop my life from disintegrating.

In response to the stress of her situation, Mary took to smoking again. In the succeeding years it steadily increased, until she was smoking twenty or more cigarettes each day. Although it became an important aid for her, and other than the Scottish country dancing her only remaining pleasure, it was a source of irritation and anxiety to me. As she deteriorated she became more careless, and liable to drop lighted cigarettes from her unsteady hand. I constantly feared that she would burn holes in the carpets or set the house on fire.

Cigarette smoking is thought to be an effective anti-depressant with less harmful side effects than prescribed drugs. In spite of knowing this, I demanded that she confine her smoking to the kitchen, so as to minimise the risk of damage, and to limit the smoke to this one part of the house. But, my intolerance was so great, that I would often discomfort her by insisting upon opening the door and windows in order to disperse the smoke. In fact, although she continued to smoke, she caused only two very minor burns in the kitchen. The memory of my unkindness towards her gives me constant cause for regret.

* * *

In the late summer of 1979 we were planning an overseas holiday, and it became necessary for us to have a number of inoculations. I did not expect Mary to show any initiative in the preparations. I had come to know that she could manage only routine matters. Therefore, it was a delightful surprise when she made appointments for the inoculations without any prompting from me. For a brief moment I was borne up by this support, and I remembered how we had shared all the routine responsibilities before the disease had struck. But as these memories rapidly faded, my renewed despair felt even more painful, because of the glimpse that I had been given of our former lives together.

Soon afterwards, I had a related but inexplicable experience. I was sitting indoors and Mary was standing with her back to a window. Sunlight was streaming in from behind, producing a halo round her head. We were talking desultorily, but as we did so she changed to become Mary as she had been before the inception of the disease. It was a beatific vision, although she was no more than the Mary whom I had known. For long minutes the illusion lingered, as in speech and appearance she was restored to me. I loved her dearly then and longed to hold her, but I dared not. I knew that this metamorphosis was ephemeral, and would disappear the moment that I moved.

When it did pass, I felt devastated. With greater clarity than any clinical observations, my 'vision' had demonstrated to me that the Mary I had married was no more, and that she only existed in my memory. After this experience I no longer questioned why my love for her was nearer to pity, and why our relationship was steadily changing from that of husband and wife, towards one of adult and dependent child.

* * *

Mary's inability to make all but the simplest decisions created various problems. She never failed to manage the shopping for food, but she was unable to buy her own clothes. She would stand agonising silently over the items of clothing presented to her, shifting uneasily from foot to foot as she strove to keep her balance, and quite unable to make a choice. For years I had bought some of her clothing at stores where goods could be exchanged, or returned, if they were unsuitable. I merely had to extend this practice.

Buying shoes for Mary was different. She needed new pairs quite frequently, because her gait caused her to kick them out at the toes and to scuff them along the insides. But unlike clothes, when I bought shoes, it was necessary to have her with me to ensure a proper fit. She would try on pair after pair, unable to make a decision, until unsympathetic sales girls would begin to show irritation. She would be silent and inarticulate, as I conscientiously ran my fingers over her feet, to determine if shoes fitted, and tried to get a reply to my searching questions, "Do they pinch anywhere? Do they feel comfortable?"

Her incapacity to buy shoes involved me in a notable altercation in a shoe shop. She had to go for a pre-holiday inoculation to the Hospital for Tropical Diseases in Central London. She travelled alone and set off early on the appointed day, but she did not return until late in the evening. It had been a day of mishaps. She had taken the wrong tube train to the hospital, in spite of having my written directions, and she arrived after the Yellow Fever session had ended. When she had explained how far she had travelled and why she was late, they had agreed to give her the inoculation. It is probable that the hospital staff could see that she was sick and incapable of coping with the London Underground system, so they had broken their routine. This had occupied her all morning.

In the afternoon she had gone shopping in Oxford St., but not before taking more wrong trains en route. She had entered a shoe shop and apparently made the assistant take out many shoes, but she had been unable to choose which pair to buy. It was a repetition of scenes that I had witnessed before and described above, but this time she was alone. Sensitive to the growing impatience of the sales girl, Mary had panicked and bought a pair that did not fit. She had finished her outing by walking round the West End in the evening, pretending, as she had expressed it, that she was normal, like all the other strollers and window-shoppers.

In the following week, I returned the shoes to the shop and asked for a refund. At first it had been refused, but when I entered into an angry tirade against the manageress, protesting that my wife had made a mistake in buying the shoes because she had Huntington's chorea, and she had the disease because of social irresponsibility, I was hurriedly paid. I was too angry at the time to be aware of anything more than my own sense of injustice. But, I doubt if a sense of justice influenced the woman. With the shop full of customers and the shoes unworn, she had given the refund to be rid of me.

* * *

Mary often seemed unaware that many of the difficulties that arose were a result of her inability to organise her life. She would be bland

and apparently content for periods lasting several days. In my feverish state, this seeming indifference to our predicament would arouse my resentment, and eventually I would explode with anger against her. She would react by saying that she had no wish to continue living, and that she was perfectly aware of what she had to do.

In the autumn of 1979, she had a very distressing experience that gave me an important insight into her state of mind. She went to a dress shop in the High St., and following a fruitless hour or two in which she was unable to decide what to buy, the manageress ordered her to leave, accusing her of not only hanging around that day, but also the previous day. Faced this time with public shame and embarrassment, Mary had angrily retorted, saying that she had Huntington's chorea, which was not her fault, and that one day the manageress might find herself with a similarly terrible disease.

I reacted with indignation to her story, and very nearly went to the shop in order to admonish the manageress for her cruel intolerance towards Mary. Meanwhile, Mary clung to me weeping uninhibitedly, showing more emotion than I had seen for months. But, even as she pressed herself to me seeking comfort and support, I was rigid and unyielding. Although my arms encircled her, she sensed the distance between us and pushed me away. I was rejecting her just as so many other people did, and she knew it. In spite of feeling guilty and of wishing to share her suffering, I could not do so. I was fearful of losing my own integrity in such a catastrophic situation. At that moment I realised her apparent indifference was, in fact, a stoically brave defence, that enabled her to live through each day without weakening and constantly breaking down.

Mary was never to have the loving care that she needed. Her lonely Via Dolorosa was to continue until she brought it to an end with a brave act that in its rational humanity and love for me, was clearly noble beside the megalomaniacal sacrifice made by the God of the Christian church.

* * *

For much of the first year following Mary's diagnosis, I was inundated by the many events that followed from it, hardly able to integrate them. We continued, too, to fill our leisure time with a busy round of activities. Despite these distractions, the conviction steadily grew that I had a moral responsibility to publicise the existence of Huntington's chorea, and to arouse public conscience so that effective action might be taken to eliminate it. It was no more than chance that I had become Mary's husband, but it seemed to be a pre-ordained fate to which I must respond.

It was not until August that I stirred myself into action and wrote to James Wilkins, the Member of Parliament for West Middlesex. In my first lengthy letter, I outlined the nature of the disease, the manner of its transmission, the numbers of afflicted people and those at risk to it in Britain, what I knew of the 'conspiracy of silence' surrounding the disease, and its continuing transmission. I asked him to take action in the direction of legislation to make it mandatory for all affected families to be sterilised. I also outlined Mary's future as a victim of the disease, and wrote of the need for the law to be changed so that she could, if she chose, receive euthanasia when she no longer wished to continue living. I enclosed with my letter some literature issued by The Euthanasia Society.

He replied promptly, and thanked me for writing about matters 'which are clearly of the greatest public importance'. He wrote, 'Conditions as horrifying as this one should not, in advanced Western societies, be allowed to become widespread'. He added, that his 'inclination was against the legislation of euthanasia'. He said he would, 'have to take professional medical advice and consult the opinion of colleagues'.

Eleven weeks and three days later, not having heard from him, I wrote again to ask if he had consulted with medical colleagues, and if he saw the need for voluntary euthanasia to be introduced.

His reply was by return post. He affirmed that he was against euthanasia, but he promised that he would write to the Minister for Health regarding Huntington's chorea. He did not give any reasons for being against voluntary euthanasia in reply to the reasoned arguments in my first letter, and I suspected, that in writing to the Minister for Health, he was attempting to avoid responsibility for answering those parts of my letter which dealt with Huntington's chorea.

Four weeks later, he sent me a copy of the reply that he had received from the Minister of State for Health. Half of this reply dealt with the facts of the disease, and for James Wilkins, must have been little more than a confirmatory reiteration of that which he had already learned from my own letter. There was one interesting paragraph which quoted government statistics, revealing that there was a relative increase of the disease in the U.K. during the first seventy years of this century. The letter also mentioned the availability of genetic counselling, contraception, and adoption for people at risk, all of which were entirely irrelevant for Mary and me, and in view of the Minister's own statistics regarding the relative increase of the disease, patently ineffective in helping to eliminate it. The letter ended with a suggestion that James Wilkin's constituent could 'contact Fight for support and advice'. This referral was an example of the unwitting role of Fight in helping authorities to avoid responsibility for eliminating the disease, a subject which I have already mentioned.

Attached to the Minister's letter was a short note from Wilkins which included, 'I think that you will find the Minister's letter both interesting and helpful'. Apart from the paragraph dealing with the increase of the disease, I found it neither. I was surprised that James Wilkins had the effrontery to think that it would.

Accordingly, I replied to him late in December, and sent a copy, and copies of my previous letters, to the Minister for Health. I wrote, that the Minister's academic detachment, whilst at the same time admitting the ineffectiveness of present day arrangements to curb the disease, was reprehensible, and that had the disease been infectious, and he, or a member of his family at risk to developing it, he would be quick to take effective action to control it. I stated that the Minister's letter was a bland abdication of responsibility, and that I still expected him (James Wilkins) to take action. I continued, by expressing disappointment that he disagreed, without giving reasons, with voluntary euthanasia. I reminded him of Mary's dreadful position, and how she would end in a mental institution, if she allowed the disease to take its course.

Wilkins replied early in January with an acknowledgement slip, saying that he would consider the points that I had made.
Six weeks and three days later, and not having heard further I wrote a short note to him, requesting an answer.

He replied early in March, saying that, having referred the matter to the Minister, there was nothing more that he could reasonably do. He added the hope that Fight could assist me.

I replied immediately, disagreeing with him that there was nothing more he could do. This implied, that in his chosen profession as a Member of Parliament he was nothing more than a rubber stamp playing games at Westminster, and that Parliament was a fiction having no control over the lives of British citizens. I continued, by writing that present day legal arrangements, either by the absence of laws to control Huntington's chorea, or the existence of laws to penalise voluntary euthanasia, were the responsibility of Parliament. I wrote that Parliamentary control, in the form of legislation, protected the innocent from assault or murder, but no legislative control existed to protect the unborn from inheriting Huntington's chorea, with consequences for them at least as bad as, and usually worse than, those suffered by a thug's victim. I ended my letter by writing, that to recommend Fight to me was useless, because the society condoned the transmission of the disease.

James Wilkins never replied. Throughout the correspondence, in which I had to remind him twice to reply to my letters following long silences, he failed to take any personal responsibility. As my Member of Parliament it was his job to do so. He chose instead to refer me evasively to Fight, and to write to the Minister, whose own abdication of responsibility he did not challenge. At no time did he offer any arguments in answer to my letters, in order to justify his own inaction.

It will be no surprise to readers to be told that the Minister for Health never replied to my copy letter. Although it was addressed to James Wilkins, it was a strong challenge to his letter.

I concluded from this correspondence, that party political expediency and personal career considerations primarily motivate our representatives at Westminster.

* * *

Shortly after starting my correspondence with Wilkins yet another of the coincidences that occur in my story, took place. For many years I had helped the local branch of the R.S.P.C.A., and I regularly took one of the secretaries to committee meetings. I knew that her husband had died a year or two earlier, following a long illness.

As usual, following the meeting, we sat in my car outside her house talking for a few minutes, prior to her going indoors. I happened to mention, that because Mary was ill, I would have to resign from the committee at some time in the future. (I did formally resign from the Chairmanship one year later, and I steadily withdrew from Branch activities in the ensuing months. I had never devoted my life to animal welfare, as some people do, but, in a charitable cause that receives no public aid, the loss of my modest commitment was another deplorable consequence of the disease.) I added that Mary suffered from Huntington's chorea, fully expecting that she would ask what it was, and I would then have to explain the nature of the disease. Instead, her eyes opened wide with surprise and she exclaimed, "That is what killed my husband!"

Her story was remarkable. She had never heard of the disease when she married, neither did she have any inkling that her husband was at risk of an hereditary disorder. She estimated that he was forty when the disease struck. From that age he steadily deteriorated in both mind and body, with all the classical symptoms, including chorea, lack of balance, and mental disturbance. Throughout the years from the onset of the disease until he died, the doctors, whom he had seen, failed to inform her that he suffered from Huntington's chorea.

She said that the last seven years of her ordeal had been the worst. Her husband had become careless in his dress and personal hygiene. He looked, as she expressed it, like a tramp, and this had drawn the disapproval of friends and relatives who had drifted away from her. In the later years, he was frequently irritable, and he often struck her.

After seventeen long years, when many people would have fled from the situation, she became suicidal. When this became apparent to a friend, he had pressed the family doctor to arrange for her husband to go into hospital. This had been agreed as a temporary measure, in order to give her a rest. Her husband had been taken to a psychiatric hospital, but he was never discharged. After three and a half weeks, he had died there. He was still able to walk, albeit with difficulty, when he was admitted, so Ellen was inclined to believe that his death was due to an influenza epidemic which had killed nine patients at that time. Perhaps the hospital authorities had rightly refrained from treating him with an anti-biotic in view of his condition.

What had not been speculative was the cause of death entered upon the death certificate. It was down as Huntington's chorea. She had finally learned the truth about her husband's disease. Subsequently she had made her own inquiries. These confirmed that all the symptoms her husband had presented, during those seventeen years, fitted the diagnosis made at the hospital. In addition, she discovered that her husband had inherited the disease from his mother.

She had two daughters and several grandchildren, but they were not biologically related to her husband. He was found to be sterile soon after marriage, so one daughter had been adopted and the other conceived by artificial insemination. It was, then, mere chance, that the conspiracy of silence and the careless attitude of doctors, had not led to immense suffering for two more generations of people.

I was sickened by the story, and I asked her, "Had you known from the onset of the disease that it was Huntington's chorea, would you have stood by him?"

"That's a difficult question", she replied, unable to answer me.

It was late, and we parted, but as I drove home my conviction that I must devote myself to eliminating the disease was strengthened. It seemed to be unavoidable.

* * *

At times I would experience a state of near-panic when I thought about the future. I knew that there was no possibility of my enduring ten, fifteen, or twenty years in the situation, each year more difficult than the previous one, as my friend had with her husband. A mere two years had passed since the disease had started, but already our lives were almost unbrokenly miserable, and would be unimaginably worse in succeeding years. I could not come to terms with the disease, as a neighbour had suggested I might eventually do. Huntington's chorea is not a stable affliction, and each day seemed to bring a fresh problem. I could not see Mary through to the stage when she could no longer be managed at home, and putting her into an institution was unthinkable. That would be the worst outcome that I could imagine.

At the time, I said to a friend that the ideal course would be to care for Mary until she could no longer be supported at home, and then to take her life when she was not expecting it. How many people would be capable of such heroic action, in which they would sacrifice many years of their lives, and then suffer arrest, trial, and imprisonment by bringing about the death of their spouse? But, in a society with a careless absence of humane legal and caring arrangements, this impossibly ideal course was the only honourable one available to me.

I began to dwell upon flight as the only practical escape from the dilemma that had been thrust upon me. Remaining with Mary could only be a temporary arrangement, and the longer I stayed the further Mary would deteriorate into helpless dependency.

In this state of mind, the approaching holiday was in the nature of a diversion away from the titanic difficulties that I faced alone. Those friends who remained were either too superficial to understand the problems, or they were unwilling to acknowledge their existence. Generally, I found that isolation was easier to bear than the frustrations created by friendships that were fictitious.

* * *

My preparations for the South African trip were slow and laborious. I did not have my usual pre-holiday enthusiasm. This was, in part, because I feared to be alone with Mary for a whole month. When I thought ahead to the problems that always arise on a foreign holiday of the type that we were about to undertake, I experienced a loss of confidence that I had never known before.

Mary attempted to pack her own bag, but when I saw that she was unable, through indecision, to complete the task, I quietly did it for her. She made no comment, and this signified how aware she was of the condition to which she had been reduced.

During the holiday, I was forced to do almost everything unaided by Mary. I hardly bothered to consult her when decisions had to be made regarding routes, overnight stops, and places to visit. I found that it was necessary to choose her meals in restaurants, in order to obviate the long periods of indecision whilst she pored over menus.

In spite of the difficulties, the holiday was a success. We led a simple life, and South Africa was a very well organised country in which to travel, so few problems arose. We had taken a tent and we hired a car, and the country's excellent campgrounds and empty roads ensured that we enjoyed a trouble-free holiday.

* * *

Mary seemed to age before my eyes when we returned to London. She had begun losing weight following the diagnosis, and her face had steadily changed to become worn and tense. In South Africa she had temporarily lost this appearance. With the holiday over and Pandora's box empty even of hope, the inevitable crises that I have written of above recurred two or three times every week. I always set them off. My fear and frustration, as I watched Mary slowly deteriorate, fed my anger. It was contradictory, that just when I most needed her support, the erosion of her mind made her incapable of giving any. She was childlike, and the vague expression on her face, that is so typical of victims of this disease, sickened me.

There was, too, the indifference shown to our situation by people around us, who often clung to the very beliefs and opinions that allowed the continuing transmission of the disease and had led to Mary's birth.

This fear and frustration produced a further and decisive erosion of our marriage in the months that followed the holiday. In the previous year, I had slipped into the belief that it would be preferable to die in my sleep, or unexpectedly in an accident, than to continue living. Seeing no end to the hardly bearable trap that I felt myself to be in, a loss of commitment to Mary, when I mentioned the future, began to enter my speech.

Mary reacted with renewed despair to these intimations of desertion that left her without a vestige of hope. She also took a practical step in the direction of self-immolation during the spring of 1980, when she telephoned the office of The Euthanasia Society in order to tell her story, and to ask for help.

* * *

Meanwhile, following a particularly bitter tirade from me earlier in the year, Mary had made her way to her brother's family once more, to seek relief from my rage. She had too much good sense to throw herself upon friends. She was aware that the initial novelty for them would be unlikely to last, and the general loosening of ties with friends, that had already taken place, was a clear indication of this. It was doubtful if she gained much comfort from these occasional flights to her family. The situation in her brother's household was hardly preferable to our own. At best Jim's family were less intemperate in reacting to their plight than I was to mine.

A major problem for Mary was the irreconcilable fact, that, although she needed me, and had no wish to continue living without me in any circumstances, I was, month by month, becoming unable to tolerate her. In escaping from me, she was temporarily relieved of the fear and confusion produced by my bombardments of anger, but it took her away from the only person for whom she really cared.

Her flight had been at a weekend, and on Sunday Judy, Roy and Catrina had taken her to evening service at a United Reformed church. When the catastrophe had broken they had taken to church-going. Previously they had been a secular family, but as Mary said to me at the time, the church-going was a form of 'hiding' from the disease, and ignoring the facts of its mode of transmission. They were avoiding their personal responsibilities as so many people involved with religion do, by putting their trust upon their creation of 'God'.

Worse was to follow for Mary. Her nephew Roy, whilst driving her home later that evening, asserted that, when he married his fiancé Catherine, whom he had met at the church, he intended to have children. He told Mary that because he was in the hands of Jesus, even if he had inherited the disease and passed it on to his children, it would not matter. It was a renewed assertion of what we had heard from his sisters in the previous August.

We were disturbed by this confirmation of a proposal that, if carried out, would effectively wreck the lives of more innocent people in the future. Inevitably my reaction, spurred by the suffering that the disease had brought to Mary and me, was to think how best to deter him from his avowed course. To confront Roy personally was impossible. Faced with a reiteration of his proposal to burden others with the suffering that had been imposed upon us, I would immediately become angry. It had to be something else. Perhaps an approach to his fiancé? No, I could not imagine myself talking to a young woman who probably had an idealised view of her future husband. The Minister of the Church, then? Yes, it would have to be him. I would have to forget my pride and approach a minister of religion, a man with a view of life unsympathetic, and even antipathetic, to my own. I would have to risk humiliation and more stress, but I was comforted by the knowledge that it would be minor and inconsequential compared with the suffering that I might avert.

But these considerations rapidly became irrelevant. The idea having occurred to me, I knew that I would despise myself if I failed to act. It was easier to see this man than to avoid doing so. I could hardly complain about the society that had endowed Mary with the disease, if I, personally, was unprepared to do everything in my power to eliminate it.

He was away when I first attempted to make contact, and several weeks passed before I was able to speak to him by telephone to ask for a meeting. At first, he was reluctant to see me because I would not disclose the reason for my request. He suggested that, if I had a problem, it would be more appropriate to see the minister of my own church. I then insisted that it was he, personally, to whom I must speak to. He explained to me afterwards, that often his time was wasted by anonymous callers, but sensing the urgency in my voice he had agreed to meet me.

I felt decidedly uneasy on that afternoon in April 1980, when I walked up the vicarage path. I knew that I must try hard to remain calm, should he prove to be unreceptive, or even hostile, towards the purpose of my visit. He was neither, and from the moment that he invited me into his home, my task became easy.

Fred Chance was a young man, hardly more than thirty, unprepossessing, and ready to listen. I had anticipated that he would know little or nothing about the disease, and so I had decided that it might be confusing for him if I were to ramble on with a disorderly exposition. Instead, I read my correspondence with Wilkins and the Minister. It was succinct, and it covered all the essential facts about the disease and the moral issues that surround it. I then went on to explain that my nephew was at risk to the disease, and that he avowed that he would have children. I finished by asking him to do everything that he could to dissuade Roy from his intentions.

Plainly, he was surprised at everything that I had related to him. He had never heard of Huntington's chorea, and it followed that he did not know that the scourge was hanging over Roy. He expressed thanks to me for informing him. He explained that he would have officiated at the wedding of my nephew and his fiancé in ignorance of the implications of their union, with Roy at a one-in-two chance of developing the disease. He wondered if Catherine had been told. He was also concerned about her family, because in his experience something relatively minor, such as concealment of one partner being an adoptee, could cause trouble when it was revealed at a later date. Indubitably, he thought that it would be very harmful to conceal the disease. He was critical and dismissive of Wilkin's evasive letters. He agreed with me that Roy should not have children, and he promised to do his best to dissuade him.

He was the first public figure to respond favourably to me. He did not know it, but my morale was raised, if only temporarily. Alas, hardly more than a year later he evaded the moral issue that I had clearly placed before him. Although he had unreservedly agreed with me that people at risk to Huntington's chorea should not have children, when my nephew's marriage drew near, he would not take the moral stand that was plainly his duty as a man and the head of a community.

Chapter 7

When Mary telephoned the The Euthanasia Society, which had changed its name to Release, she spoke to Leslie Ford, the General Secretary. Leslie, I learned later, was a young man in his early thirties who had been appointed Secretary in April, 1978. With great energy and enthusiasm, he was transforming the old, rather lethargic E.S., into a lively crusading movement. The proposed publication and distribution to Release members of a Guide which set out information on various acceptable methods of suicide, was largely the result of his own initiative and organising ability.

I was also to learn later, without surprise, that he was constantly under the pressure of letters and telephone calls from desperate or despairing people like Mary, or their friends and relatives, who turned to Release for help or advice, because there were no other agencies to which the intolerably sick, who were unwilling to continue living, could turn.

Without wishing to intrude on her conversations I had heard her weeping into the telephone when she spoke, at first to Leslie, and then to a second man, called Len. Len telephoned Mary several times following her calls to Leslie. Mary said that Len was prepared to come to the house to assist her suicide, whilst I went away for a weekend. It seemed quite fantastic to me at the time, and I could not believe what was proposed. On one occasion Mary wanted me to speak to Leslie, but I refused, saying that I would have nothing to do with the proposal.

Mary always referred to Len as her only friend, and this led me to believe that he and Leslie were operating a 'Samaritan'–type line. At his request, I spoke only once to Len, for just five minutes. At first, my vulnerable emotional state led me to talk candidly about my fears and misery, but in reply he spoke very strangely about re-incarnation, expressing noticeable enthusiasm for suicide, in principle. He hinted at that course for me, because he thought I might not find life worthwhile, or even possible, if or when, Mary died. My candour dried up immediately, and I felt humiliated when his eccentricity became plain.

I am surprised, now, that I did not take Mary's conversations with Len more seriously. I was simply unable to believe that his proposal to assist her suicide was sincere. It appeared at the time to be no more than another expression of his eccentricity, but I was wrong.

* * *

Early in the evening of a day in May, a new and remarkable dimension was added to the 'nightmare' in which we lived. Three men dressed like salesmen, in dark pin-striped suits came to our door. One of them quoted our telephone number asking me to confirm it. 'What', I momentarily thought, 'are they selling telephones or something?' But before my thoughts could take me further, they produced identity badges, and stated that they were C.I.D. officers. Immediately, I thought that I must have unknowingly witnessed a road accident, which they were investigating. But again, before I could consider this fresh possibility one of them asked if I had ever spoken to Martin Smith.

"No", I replied puzzled, "I've never heard the name before".

Even as I started to reason that obviously they were mistaken in coming to me with their questions, and that it was clearly a case of wrong identity, the next question came rapidly.

"But you are a member of the Voluntary Euthanasia Society?" My mind raced and sharpened.

"Yes", I replied, "I am a member of the Euthanasia Society, but I've never spoken to Martin Smith, only to Leslie Ford".

"You have", one of the trio quickly and heavily countered. I remained silent, resisting an urge to reply, 'Then why ask me, if you already know'.

One of the three next produced a clip-board and proceeded to read extracts from a paper on it. They were quotations from conversations that could only have taken place over the telephone between Mary and someone connected to the E.S.. They included details of a house-key that we customarily left hidden beneath our front garden hedge, and a sentence or two by Mary concerning our dog, and the daily walks that she gave him.

At that moment I knew that our telephone had been monitored, and that Len must, in fact, be Martin Smith. In retrospect, I am surprised that in spite of this startling realisation I remained cool, my face showing at most icy hostility towards the police.

The tall, thin member of the trio then began to speak irritably and aggressively. It appeared that their interviewing technique was to lead with unnerving statements, but before the interviewee could regain composure, to press on with their demands or questions.

"We want to question your wife", he said.

"Why?" I asked, feeling at a distinct disadvantage, because at that time I did not have even rudimentary knowledge of my legal rights in such a situation.

"We are tying up loose ends", was the testy reply.

In part because of my ignorance, in part curiosity, after a few more brief exchanges I went for Mary and led her to the door. As we reached it, I said acidulously and with heavy irony, "These three 'gentlemen' are from the C.I.D., and they have been tapping our 'phone. They wish to question you".

Mary was confused and frightened, but so unforthcoming that the police quickly lost interest and left. The dark one, a Detective Chief Inspector

Mayhew, to my surprise, left his card so that we could, 'contact him to give information in the future'. His optimism, in view of our undisguised hostility, was very ill-founded.

It was yet another coincidence, that this doorstep interview with the C.I.D. took place only minutes before we left for the theatre to see a production of 'Whose Life Is It Anyway?' by Brian Clark. From an encounter with the police, in which we had learned that Mary's move to find the only way out of the trap in which society had placed her had led to our telephone being monitored, we went straight to a powerful statement of the obstacles placed in the way of a man paralysed by a broken neck, to frustrate his wish to die. The play alone was so clear in its relevance to Mary's position, that we would have been shaken by it, but to have the two experiences within the space of one evening left us dazed, when we returned home.

* * *

Sleep that night was impossible, as the implications of the telephone tapping accumulated in our minds. Minute by minute its horror grew. We did not know for how long the police had been listening to us. We knew from the extracts quoted by them that it had been done at least throughout May. We were then at the end of the month. Vainly we struggled to remember all the intimate or significant conversations that we had made during recent months. We needed to know just how much that was damaging or revealing, had been spoken over the telephone. In my feverish state of mind, I feared that it might be stored in a state computer bank, always available for instant recall by the police or government agencies. We had been caught in a surveillance net of a type that we associated only with the regimes that are east of the 'Iron Curtain', or in Latin America. It served to give us a little understanding of the personal and social damage, which is caused by fear, in those states where police activities are unbridled.

Bitter and outraged, I realised how casual and unguarded the spoken word is likely to be because of its ephemeral nature. By contrast, the most intimate of diaries or letters is less likely to lift the seventh veil, because the written word is tangible and permanent. In future neither of us could use our telephone other than for the most innocuous of calls. This would be a serious deprivation for Mary, because she was less mobile now that she was not allowed to drive, and the telephone was an important link with her remaining friends.

Throughout the long years of Mary's suffering, the period following the C.I.D. visit was the only one in which she lost all her control and became distraught, even frenetic at times, rolling wildly on the floor and screaming. Leslie Ford and Martin Smith had presented her with the most reasonable escape from her frightful position; an assisted suicide, but abruptly, and in the foulest manner, it had been denied to her. She felt trapped, and condemned to deteriorate to a helpless wreck, unless she was able to organise her own release, a far more difficult undertaking, fraught with the risk of failure. This interference by the forces of the State, was, in temporal terms, to double Mary's suffering.

Long after midnight on that memorable night, our need to talk with someone and to pour out our story was so strong, that we drove round to a friend who lived nearby. Our telephone call to warn her of our arrival, fortunately, or so she may have tactfully said, found her reading in bed and not asleep. She did her best for us. She listened to our story and provided coffee, but in spite of her warmth, I sensed that she was more flattered and pleased that we had turned to her, than able to give us the positive support and help that we needed.

* * *

The next morning I went up to the Release office, with the intention of warning Leslie Ford. I could not telephone; undoubtedly their telephone was also being monitored. When I arrived, he was not there. I was told by other members of the small staff that he was away on holiday and would not return until the following week. I arranged to call again after the weekend. Before leaving I warned them that the C.I.D. were investigating Release, that my telephone had been tapped, and that it was likely that theirs was, also.

The following Wednesday I went again to the Release office, and this time Leslie was present. I told him about the police visit, and added that, during the past week, the C.I.D. had repeatedly rung Mary during the day asking her for an interview. I continued by telling him that these calls, following the police visit, had reduced her to such a dread of the telephone that she had stopped answering it. She was also fearful of answering a knock at the door, and I had advised her always to check who was there before opening it, in case the C.I.D. made a second visit. I explained to Leslie, that in addition, the police had traced me to my office, telephoning me like Mary, and pressing for an interview.

In view of this harassment, Leslie rang Martin Smith's solicitors from the Release office for their advice. (Martin Smith had been arrested May 27th). After a brief explanatory conversation he passed the receiver to me. A very taciturn man, presumably believing, like me, that our words were being monitored, advised me that we did not have to comply with the requests for an interview, and to ignore them.

Mary did answer the telephone in the following week, and she did agree to give the C.I.D. an interview, but after pausing to allow them time to respond eagerly, she added that it must be conducted in her solicitor's office! Her wit brought the harassment to an end. They never telephoned again.

* * *

In addition to warning Leslie and the staff at the Release office, I also warned my colleagues to be careful when they used the office telephone. When I added that the root cause of all these unpleasant events was

Huntington's chorea, and that everyone at risk should be sterilised, I received a remarkable reply from one of them.

He disagreed, saying, "After all, people have forty or fifty years of life before it is triggered off".

Ignorance about the nature of Huntington's chorea could not excuse his statement, for I had explained the salient points about the disease to my colleagues, and he had seen the Fight T.V programme, which was sufficiently informative to convey the horror of the disease.

I was reminded of those friends who showed reluctance to agree that affected people should be sterilised, but who barely concealed their disapproval of my intolerance of Mary, which was a direct result of the disease. These same people often overlooked the failings in their own marriages to healthy spouses.

I replied, that people with his opinions should be made to bear the responsibility for their results, and care for the victims of the disease. To this definitive statement he was unable to reply.

* * *

Mary's anguish at this time was, as I have written, extreme. Frightened by her expressions of desperation and feeling helpless, I attempted to find a social worker to visit her. I could not approach the Hilton Area Health Authority and risk their sending Mrs King, or one of her assistants. So instead, I telephoned an adjacent A.H.A., which employed a neighbour who had warmly praised one of their social workers. He was reputed to be very well-informed on Huntington's chorea and its problems.

He was not available when I made the call, so I left a suitable message for him. I feared that he would be unwilling, or unable, to work in another health authority area, and the message would be passed to Hilton. My supposition was correct. A few days later, a letter came from the Hilton A.H.A. Inviting me to contact them. Mary had, by then, emerged from the acutely desperate state that she had experienced during the period following the police visit. I replied tersely, stating that, if necessary, we would contact them.

The police interference and harassment also had the effect of arousing my own aggressive anger even further, and consequently Mary was also subjected to more violent tirades from me throughout June and July. She once stayed out all night wandering the streets while I sat up sleepless, following one crisis with all the usual recriminations from me. A few days later we had another frightful scene, which was notable because, for the first time after eighteen months of my anger, she justifiably accused me of 'letting her down'.

Following a particularly bitter tirade from me early in July, Mary fled in tears once more, but on this occasion it was to a friend. Morag invited her to stay overnight, and the next morning telephoned me to suggest that Mary remain with her for a few days to give us both a respite. I agreed to this arrangement because I needed to be away from Mary, but I felt resentful because it was nothing more than a temporary expedient that was being offered, in a situation with which I could not cope. Until the onset of the disease, excepting two weeks when I had been obliged by my employer to attend courses away from home, one short period when Mary had been in hospital, and once when I had visited a sick brother, we had never spent a night apart throughout the years of our marriage.

Following the telephone call, I remembered an aphorism spoken by a friend many years earlier, 'When a marriage is going, it's gone'. I knew that, even if some means had been found by medical science at that time to halt the progress of the disease, it would be too late to save our marriage.

Mary did not, after all, stay with Morag. A party of us had pre-arranged to go to a Scottish country dance that evening, and when we returned to Morag's house, it became so obvious that Mary wanted to be with me, that the proposal was dropped. Whatever my feelings were, there was no doubt that Mary needed me, and no conceivable arrangements that a caring society might make for her could be effective, if I were excluded from them.

* * *

Late in July, Mary had an unexpected visit from a Hilton A.H.A. social worker, who stated that she was calling in response to a complaint to her office from a neighbour, about disturbances from our house and Mary being seen leaving in tears. Undoubtedly, this was because of the frequency and pitch of the verbal violence brought on by events since May. Whatever the motive of the Social Services office in sending a representative to see Mary, its effect was harmful, because it made us feel that we were being watched by neighbours, and it did not give the slightest help to Mary.

My anger, caused by Mrs King's outrageous interference in the previous year, was renewed when this unsolicited visit was made. Following Mrs. King's visit, I had written to the Director of Social Services, to inform him that if I wanted a social worker I would ask for one through the local health visitor. This time I felt impelled to write to the Chairman of the Hilton Social Services Committee. I enclosed a copy of my letter of complaint about Mrs. King, which on the advice of local health visitors had not been sent.

I wrote that, following the monitoring of our telephone and police harassment, my wife's distress was so acute that I had contacted the Brentham A.H.A. but they had passed my request to Hilton, and following the consequent letter from Hilton, I had written to make it clear that I would ask for a social worker, if I required one.

This latest uninvited social worker, had told my wife that she was there because a neighbour had complained about angry scenes, and my wife being seen leaving the house in distress. I continued, that this may be true, but it was hardly surprising, in view of my wife's disease which society was responsible for thrusting on to us. In addition, there was the telephone tapping, the C.I.D. harassment, and other related difficulties, including the cruelly tactless statements made by Mrs. King, none of these being conducive towards marital harmony. My wife did not have visits from neighbours, therefore this informer was a hypocrite to contact Social Services whilst not giving my wife any help.

I expressed surprise that the Social Services encouraged informers, and that this particular worker tactlessly mentioned the complaint, in order to justify her visit. It appeared, I added, that social workers are primarily concerned to 'get the paper work right', the people they visit being of secondary importance.

I reminded the Chairman that I had never asked for a visit from a Hilton social worker, and that in two letters I had made it clear that I would contact their office if I needed one.

I concluded the letter by writing that all contacts with the Social Services in Hilton had resulted in additional distress for my wife, and asked the Chairman to instruct the Director of Social Services to stay away in future, unless my wife or I asked for help.

The Chair of the Committee never replied to my letter, instead she passed it to the Social Services office for acknowledgement. One month later, the Director of Social Services briefly wrote to say that no further attempt would be made to contact us, unless our circumstances changed, or a specific request was made by either of us for assistance.

This literary fracas illustrates the accumulation of problems that may ensue, if one has the misfortune to suffer disease or accident. It also

101

demonstrates the incompetence of the local A.H.A.. It was, too, an example of the waste of my time and energy fighting to retain our dignity, in the face of a society that seemed to alternate between callousness and hostility. Before 1980 ended, we were to suffer another unpleasant clash with a public organisation that was a direct result of the monitoring of our telephone and my belligerent response to it.

* * *

Within days of the social worker's unsolicited visit, and whilst its memory was fresh in my mind, I suffered more interference from a neighbour. Doris and her husband had been friendly with Mary and me in past years, but since Mary's diagnosis, when Doris had disagreed with my assertion that all families with the disease should be sterilised, I had borne her a grudge. I preferred to keep her coolly at a distance. It was similar to my reaction towards friends and acquaintances, who showed any reluctance to agree with me. My rancour towards her was strengthened for another and related reason.

She owned a setter that went blind in middle age, and the discovery was made that the condition was caused by a genetic disorder present in some strains of the breed. The mode of inheritance was identical to Huntington's chorea, that is, the defect was caused by an auto sominal dominant gene. The bitch had recently whelped two puppies, shortly before she was found to be rapidly going blind, so each pup was at a one in two chance of having inherited the gene, and itself going blind in later years.

When Doris told me about this soon after Mary's diagnosis, I unhesitatingly said that both pups should be sterilised. She disagreed, saying that she had warned the new owner of the bitch puppy and the dog puppy she had decided to keep, and he would not be allowed out alone. I reasoned with her, that if ever he picked up the scent of a bitch in season, he would ignore any recall whistle and would follow the scent until he found the bitch. The genetic disorder might then enter the local mongrel dog population, where its eradication would be almost impossible, because no pedigree records are kept.

"Why not", I pressed, "have him castrated?"

"No, certainly not", she replied.

"You could have him vasectomised, then", I added.

"No, no," came the reply, her hands ready to be raised in horror at my suggestion, "I don't want a randy dog".

Faced not only with her irresponsibility, but also with her base ignorance, I stopped trying to persuade her.

Almost two years later, and feeling mounting anger against anyone who held the opinions that had led to the slow destruction of Mary's brain, and the ruination of my own life, for the first time I ignored her when in passing she said, "Hullo, Brian". I found this was easier than acknowledging her with my customary coolness. Not receiving a reply she repeated the greeting in an aggressive tone. Then, to my surprise, she came striding across the road to where I was working in my garden, and demanded to know why I did not answer her.

There then followed a remarkable scene. I would have expressed myself most finely had I cursorily told her to 'Fuck off', but I didn't. Instead, I told her, quite simply, that I preferred to ignore her because of her opinions on Huntington's chorea, and her refusal to have the dog sterilised, and the clear link between these facts. She angrily denied that she had ever disagreed with sterilisation, but, equally hotly, I asserted that she had. From this point a row ensued which could quite easily have led to blows, especially when she had the audacity to accuse me of neglecting Mary. I retorted by saying that if she felt the slightest concern for Mary, she would have visited her during the previous two years, and that if she had no wish to meet me, any visits or invitations could have been made whilst I was at work. She replied irrationally, that she would visit Mary when she chose to, not when I did. Finally, I accused her of contacting the Hilton A.H.A.. This she vehemently denied.

Later, I felt annoyed that I had allowed myself to be drawn into such an undignified and heated exchange. This woman was exceptionally egotistical, and the demand for a reply to her greeting was motivated by pique, and probably guilt, defensively expressed as aggression for her neglect of Mary. Naturally, this incident, following the social worker's visit, increased my feeling that I was under hostile observation by neighbours.

* * *

I have already mentioned the moral abdication revealed by Fight in their failure to call for affected families to stop breeding. Their ambivalent silence was broken in May, shortly before the C.I.D. visit. I received a newsletter from the London branch of the Association, which included a proposal to arrange a discussion group for couples where one partner was at risk to the disease, in order to consider whether to have children. This was the first time I had seen Fight literature, which clearly showed that it was their policy to encourage people at risk to make their own choice, rather than to press them not to have children.

It was more than I could bear. I immediately wrote to the General Secretary of the Association. It was the most angry and vitriolic letter that I have ever written. I enclosed copies of my correspondence with James Wilkins, which adequately explained my position, and saved me the labour of repeating all the arguments that I had used to him.

I started by inviting her to read my letters, which broadly described the circumstances causing the transmission of the disease in Britain. I explained that my nephew was refusing to take personal responsibility in favour of taking refuge in religion, proclaiming that he would have children when he married. This development, plus my experience of the behaviour of other members of my wife's family and of the medical profession, encompassed most reasons for the continuation of the disease. This was why, more than a century after George Huntington's paper, there were 30,000 people at risk to the disease in Britain.

Because she must be aware of these facts, I found the role of Fight impossible to understand. I could not believe my wife and I were very different from other families, or exceptional in experiencing the disease as a personal catastrophe. Any difference must lie in our realism, and in our rejection of palliatives offered by the people around us, and by our refusal to be cajoled by fear into holding the opinions that promote the continuance of H.C..

I wrote, that in all the literature I had received from Fight and in the radio and television programmes, no one had proclaimed the simple moral imperative that people at risk must not procreate, and that this evasion was a monstrous deceit.

I claimed that the officers and members of Fight were a cosy group insulating themselves against the unpalatable fact, that, for example, their own births were not accidental. Their parents knew that there was a serious hereditary disorder in the family, or, at the very least, they did not bother to enquire why relatives ended mysteriously in mental hospitals. How much easier for them to have children in order to enter the illusion that they had not inherited the fatal gene. How easy, too, to pretend that a cure for the disease would soon be found.

I then outlined my telephone conversation with Mrs. Jenkins eighteen months earlier, when she did not react with more than, "Oh", to my complaint that Fight had not bothered to ask Jim or Mary if they had children, and did not think a 50% chance of inheritance justified sterilisation.

I asked if she had thought of the personal responsibility that she bore, as the founder and secretary of Fight, for condoning people at risk procreating. Did she realise, I continued, that buttressing people into slothful acceptance of the current situation, she must bear some blame for the catastrophes that innocent people would, as a result, suffer in the future? I also asked her to consider the immorality of using live animals in medical research into the disease, when it could easily be eliminated if families were sterilised.

I referred her to the item in which the discussion group was mentioned, and asked how she could remain secretary of an association that proposed setting up this group. I questioned whether she possessed any conscience or sense of moral responsibility, since her primary duty should be to stop, by all possible means, people at risk from procreating. I asked how she could administer an organisation that encourages people to make their own choice, and I called her a hypocrite for running Fight with the aim of helping affected families, whilst at the same time condoning transmission of the disease.

Finally, I stated, that if ever I took any part in Fight, it would be to destroy it in its present form, and to turn it into an association with the aim of eliminating the disease.

The C.I.D. visit followed a few days after posting this letter, and it stung me into writing a second letter to her before the month ended. This letter was much shorter, and in effect, a postscript to the first one.

I wrote, that we had been visited by three C.I.D. officers because of my wife's contacts with The Euthanasia Society, our telephone had been monitored, and the police had proved this by reading extracts from my wife's conversations. In addition to our disastrous situation because of my wife's condition, we were being persecuted, and my wife was unable to use our telephone. I ended by asking if this latest outrage, which was a direct result of my wife inheriting Huntington's chorea, convinced her of the moral shortcoming of Fight, which tacitly encouraged the transmission of the disease.

Little more than two weeks later I received a reply to these two letters from Rose Lock, the professional social worker employed by Fight.

She wrote that my two letters had been passed to her by the General Secretary, and that she was sorry to hear what a worrying time I was having. She understood the strain of caring for an H.C. patient, and added that it sounded as though I was carrying it alone. She explained that she had attempted to contact me by 'phone to see if she could give me any support, but had been unable to get through, and she suggested that the trouble that I had experienced with my telephone was perhaps the reason. She finished by inviting me to ring her.

This letter was a classic example of the style of approach made by many people in the psychiatric field, towards those they consider to be ill. She treated everything that I had written, as if it had no objective validity, and was merely an expression of sickness. Plainly, she considered my second letter, dealing with the monitoring of our telephone, to be pure fantasy. By employing this technique, she was able to continue in her professional role within Fight, undisturbed by any doubts regarding the moral probity of her work that might have been roused by my letters.

I did not reply. In response to my cry of protest, she had suppressed all reason and offered me a bribe. In inviting me to turn to her for support, she was also asking me to surrender my integrity.

* * *

Shortly after the C.I.D. visit, Mary wrote what was to be her last letter. It was to her old Shetland friend, Sheila, with whom she had trained, both as a nurse and a midwife. Sheila had returned to live in the Shetlands, so Mary had not seen her for several years. Sheila did not know that Mary had developed Huntington's chorea, because the most recent contact between them had taken place a few years earlier. Perhaps Mary, in her desperate and isolated state, turned to Sheila in the belief that she was the one remaining friend who might give her real support or solace.

I well remember that evening when Mary toiled for several hours to produce a letter, throwing away many sheets of writing paper before she felt satisfied with her efforts. I retrieved and kept all the discarded sheets, and before posting off the letter for her, I took a photo-copy of it. I sensed at the time that it would be her last letter, and I wanted a copy as a record.

Mary's final draft was a brief but reasonably complete outline of the salient events in our lives during the previous three years, since the inception of the disease. It was also a pitiful reflection of the damage that had already been done to her once quick and intelligent mind. It looked and read like the letter of a child, with its unsteady script and its grammatical and spelling errors.

Mary waited for a letter, or a telephone call, or even a quick visit. She always emphasised that Sheila was the closest friend that she had ever had, but Sheila never replied.

* * *

In the middle of July we received our first quarterly telephone bill since the C.I.D. visit. Normal prompt payment was impossible. The Post Office is responsible for making the technical arrangements that enable the police to monitor telephones. I could not meekly pay the bill without making some form of protest.

I returned it immediately with a covering letter, which stated that during the previous quarter, and possibly in the succeeding weeks, my telephone had been monitored by the C.I.D.. Because I had a shared line with the police, I was returning the bill to them for the appropriate reduction.

The West Telephone Area of London replied with an acknowledgement card, and then, three weeks later, a letter came from the Accounts Officer stating that he did not know why I thought that my line was being tapped by the C.I.D.. He assured me that it was an exclusive one that nobody else could use. He was returning the bill, and looked forward to receiving payment from me.

I replied by return post thanking him for his letter, and assuring him that a team of C.I.D. officers had called at my house and quoted from my wife's private telephone conversations, therefore, my telephone was shared with the police.

Back came the inevitable card from the Post Office Telecommunications, and then, a few days later, a standard letter from the Accounts Officer, saying that enquiries were still in hand and a full reply would be sent as soon as possible.

The following day I received another reminder that the account was unpaid. I replied by return post, reminding them that they had promised to send me a full reply.

Eight days later, I was sent an 'Important Notice' stating that, because my bill remained unpaid, they were about to disconnect the service. Hitherto, all communications had been politely conducted, but the Post Office were now preparing to apply naked force. I was equally determined that they would not be allowed to escape the moral responsibility that was theirs, for being part of arrangements that had enabled the police to monitor our telephone. Accordingly, I rang the accounts department and fully explained the position to a member of the staff. He left the telephone for a few minutes, and when he returned he advised me to ignore the 'Important Notice', pending a proper reply from them.

Five weeks passed, during which I was hardly able to give any thought to the unpaid telephone bill, as our lives dragged hopelessly on, our misery inadequately anaesthetised by a constant round of activities. I was therefore surprised, when I returned home one day early in October, to be told by Mary that earlier in the day she had heard a loud click from the telephone, and on lifting the receiver had found it to be 'dead'. They had carried out their threat made in August, and disconnected us.

I was enraged at this crude and forceful move that circumvented my aim of obtaining an admission from Post Office Telecommunications of their part in the monitoring of our telephone. At the first opportunity, I attempted to speak directly with the West Telephone Area General Manager, but in this I was frustrated. Although I repeatedly demanded to be connected to him, I was, instead, connected first to an accounts office, and then to a customer relations office. I was, by this time, literally shouting my story at everyone I spoke to, and demanding that my telephone be re-connected.

Not achieving the slightest helpful response from these minions of the Post Office, I wrote to the Manager and sent copies to The Postmaster General, The General Secretary of the Post Office Engineering Union, and James Wilkins, my M.P..

I began by writing that my telephone, as he must know, had, and possibly was continuing to be monitored by the C.I.D.. I knew this because they had quoted from my wife's conversations. I told him this had been done because of my wife's contacts with The Euthanasia Society, which the C.I.D. were investigating. I explained that my wife suffered from Huntington's chorea, and the country had allowed her to be born heir to this terrible fate, and was allowing the C.I.D. to persecute us precisely as a consequence of it. I accused him of being responsible, since his engineers make the technical arrangements for the monitoring of telephones. I referred him to my correspondence with the Post Office, and the failure to keep their word and send me a full reply. I also mentioned the member of the accounts department, who had advised me to ignore the 'Important Notice'. I wrote that now my telephone was disconnected, my sick wife was cut off from her friends, and when I had asked to be allowed to speak directly to him, in order to rectify this, I had been refused. I inferred from this that his policy was to avoid personal responsibility. I concluded by asking for my telephone to be restored and my letters answered, and to be informed if my telephone was continuing to be monitored.

Two days later, a representative of the Post Office contacted me to arrange a meeting at my home to discuss the telephone bill and my letter. When he arrived, his manner was a little condescending and dismissive. It was obvious that he had pre-judged me to be eccentric. After fifteen minutes of rapid explanatory talk from me, covering our situation and the events of the past few months, which substantiated my reason for not paying the bill, he became uneasy and diffident. He apologetically explained to me that invariably, when people complained that their 'phone was being tapped, it was because they heard clicks from it. Unlike the minions with whom I had argued in the previous week, he did not deny that the Post Office was responsible for the technical arrangements of telephone tapping. He added, that it was done only in serious criminal cases, or where national security was involved.

Following his loss of confidence when I disabused him of his false assumptions, he made proposals to solve the impasse. He would have the telephone re-connected, but would I please pay the bill. There was nothing more that I could achieve through him. I had made my protest, and there was also my letter of the previous week with copies sent to the Postmaster General, the Engineer's Union, and my M.P..

The following day the telephone was restored and I paid the bill. There was a minor sequel. The next quarterly bill, followed by a red reminder, came whilst we were on holiday. No deduction had been made to the rental charge for the week when the telephone had been disconnected, and the amount for the previous quarter had been included. I had evidence that the previous bill had been paid because the cheque had been cleared through my bank, but I anticipated more trouble over the rental charge for the period when the telephone had been cut off. For once my fears were unfounded. I wrote to the Post Office representative and he immediately sent me a correct bill.

These events cost me much frustration and stress, as I fought to resist the casual assumption, made by the Post Office that we were of no consequence, and must conform to arrangements on which we had not been consulted and over which we had no control. Ironically, it was at this time that we first heard that Martin Smith kept diaries which the police had appropriated. This cast doubt on our belief that our telephone had been tapped. The C.I.D. may have been quoting from these diaries, but that first evening, and again when they spoke to me at my office, I had accused them of monitoring our telephone, and they did not deny it. I raised this point with other people connected with the Ford/Smith case, as it came to be known, and, like me, they were uncertain. One acquaintance, who was a probation officer, assured me that in her experience 'phone-tapping was commonplace. She did not express surprise when I told her about our visit from the C.I.D.. Whether or not our telephone had been monitored, the effect upon us was as if it had.

* * *

Three months after Martin Smith's arrest, his solicitors wrote to me. He was held in Brixton prison on remand, and they had begun work on his defence. I was asked if I was prepared to help, and, when I agreed, an interview was arranged. Their offices were in a seedy part of Islington, and it was clear from the many notices and posters pinned up drawing attention to the individuals' civil rights, that it was a radical establishment committed to liberal ideals.

I saw a youngish woman who was not very communicative. I quickly imparted everything that I knew about Mary's contacts with Leslie and Martin Smith, and the subsequent visit by the C.I.D. and their harassment of us. I added that I hoped other people involved would not be intimidated

112

by the police, and would help in the defence. I said I feared my wife could not be of any help, because, if she were called as a witness, her evidence would only substantiate the charges against Martin Smith of aiding suicides. The solicitor agreed with me, and I left when she said she would contact us, if it was decided that we might be of assistance.

She never did, and whilst I would not have refused to help in the defence, I preferred not to be associated with a man who seemed to me to be very odd. His eccentricity was to be amply confirmed the following year.

Chapter 8

By the late summer of 1980, almost two years had elapsed since Mary had worked, and almost one year since she had completed her year of half-pay and been placed on pension. With the exception of occasional visits from an ex-colleague who had retired on medical grounds, the other nurses neither visited Mary nor telephoned her. It was not that visits would have been difficult, as local district nurses it would have been easy for them to have their morning coffee with her from time to time. Several of them actually had patients close by, or they regularly drove past our house in the course of their work.

This avoidance of Mary could not be excused on the grounds of fear or embarrassment, when faced with her condition. Mary, after three years, was still in an early stage of the disease, and not a day would pass without the district nurses seeing sick and elderly people in far worse states of health than hers. Nor could they be excused on the grounds that the disease had changed Mary's personality, to make her disagreeable. It was in part because of her cheerful demeanour and courage, both in private and public, that I received the disapprobation of friends, who lacked the imagination to understand that I continued to need less obvious qualities that the disease had eroded.

Equally painful to Mary, was her colleagues' unprecedented omission to make a collection for her retirement, when she was pensioned off. Normally, there would be a social gathering with wine, refreshments, speeches, and a presentation. This would have been inappropriate for Mary because of her circumstances, but we both expected that a collection would be made, and she would be discretely given a gift and card. It was known to everyone that she would never work again, long before her year of half-pay ended. It was for this reason that I anticipated the collection would be made well in advance of her retirement.

Nothing happened. The months passed and we entered 1980. Spring came and then summer, and it was not until late August, almost one year too late, and long after we had accepted that Mary was forgotten, that one of the nurses, single-handed made a collection for Mary. When word of the black and white portable television set, that had been bought, reached us, I wanted to refuse it, but Mary disagreed. She defiantly argued, that, having contributed over the years to many retirement presents she would "Have this out of them". When the set arrived, it was touching to see the pleasure that she derived from showing it to a visitor, with the accompanying card, embellished with signatures, propped up against it.

Long afterwards, I searched in vain for this card. Mary normally hoarded similar mementoes. I believe that her disillusionment with colleagues had led her to destroy it.

* * *

With all my annual leave to take, but fearing to go away alone with Mary, which would place us constantly together, it occurred to me that a group package tour might provide a suitable solution. Knowing, too, that she intended suicide, or that in any event the disease would preclude her from foreign holidays in the future, I decided not to be stinting regarding cost. I checked many brochures, finally selecting an 'Art Treasures Tour of India and Nepal'.

It was a five star tour, with eight internal flights, and accommodation in palatial hotels. Our party of nineteen included a very efficient courier, and an academic who gave lectures most evenings. In addition, there were guides at all the locations. But, from the moment when I first saw our fellow-travellers, I sensed that I had made a mistake. Almost all of them were older than us, and they were mostly professional people. There were, for example, four doctors of medicine and one doctor's wife. The conservative atmosphere that they collectively produced was stultifying, and I felt reduced to a cypher. Their unmoving urbanity based, in part, upon secure backgrounds so different from our own circumstances, constantly rankled with me.

We were only three days out when I was involved with two doctors in an argument about voluntary euthanasia and Huntington's chorea. Their quiet certainty in rejecting voluntary euthanasia and curbs to stop Huntington's chorea families from breeding drew an acrimonious attack from me. They believed in a continuation of the current haphazard situation, which so often makes termination of life for the intolerably sick, dependent upon individual doctors. The assertion made by these two, that it was best to leave doctors to administer the final overdose of morphine to hasten the death of the incurably ill suffering pain, was irrelevant to Mary's situation and to those similarly placed. It also revealed inconsistency, because statistics show doctors to have a very high suicide rate. Self-deliverance is considerably easier for them, because they have access to drugs and to information on their effects. This is denied to most other people. These two were silent when I said, as I had so often before, that those people who do not agree with effective radical measures to eliminate Huntington's chorea should take responsibility for the care of the disease's victims.

This publicly conducted exchange, witnessed by half of the group, tended to isolate Mary and me from the party. Perhaps they were a little fearful of me, and it is possible that, having paid substantial sums of money for the tour, they believed that it was unfair of me to display uninhibited emotion and create a divisive effect. Following that unpleasant start, all parties showed more discretion in their choice of topics for conversation.

The holiday was nearing its end when Mary and I happened to be seated for a meal with another of the doctors. He had said very little other than conventional pleasantries to us before, but on this occasion he questioned us about our situation. After listening sympathetically to our story, he said that recently he had had a patient with the disease. He added that it had been very nasty towards the end. Finally, he turned to Mary, and naming a drug which I have now forgotten said, "When you have had enough, take sixty of those. But make sure that you will not be disturbed for forty eight hours; they are very clever at reviving people these days".

* * *

Following the holiday in India, I once more entered into correspondence with my M.P., James Wilkins. This time it was set off because the Government had not increased the annual rate of Invalidity Benefit (which was paid to Mary) by the same amount as the current rate of inflation.

I started my letter by drawing his attention to this discrepancy, but continued by reminding him that my wife's condition was not accidental, but was the result of previous governments not taking action to eliminate the disease. I reminded him that it is normal in Western societies to support the weak and the sick, and for mandatory legislation to be passed to protect people's health. His refusal to take any action in response to my earlier letters, indicated that he was without the moral standards that, as a Parliamentarian, he should be foremost in upholding.

I suggested that, if saving had to be made by the Government he supported, the cost for this reduction in my wife's Invalidity Benefit should be borne by those people who, like himself, refuse to take action to eliminate the disease. I made the point that it was inconsistent of him to support a Government committed to reducing public expenditure, whilst he condoned the transmission of Huntington's chorea. The disease was a large drain on the economy through the Health and Social Services, and the pensions paid to its victims. There was also the loss to the community of skilled people like my wife, who had been trained at public expense, and the loss of relatives who leave their jobs to care for victims of the disease.

I asked him what action he would take to have the Benefit increased, and what public criticism of the policy he was prepared to make. I also asked, in view of his refusal to take any action to eliminate the disease, and his unwillingness to admit the need for voluntary euthanasia for the disease's victims, what responsibility he would take for them. What, for example, was he prepared to do to improve Health and Social Services upon which H.C. sufferers are dependent?

Finally, I assured him, that even if he accepted his responsibilities for the care of victims of the disease, he could not remove the 'nightmare' in which my wife and I lived, and this would happen to more innocent people in the future, if those at risk were not stopped from procreating.

I sent copies of this letter to the Minister of State for Health, and the Minister for Social Security.

Three days later Wilkins replied, saying that I had his personal sympathy regarding my wife's condition. He claimed that the new rate of Invalidity Benefit had been planned according to a projected lower rate of inflation. He added that the Government had spent more in real terms on the National Health Service than the previous one. He did not pretend that it was enough, but there was an urgent necessity to put the economy right, so that more resources would be available for the sick in the future.

Almost three weeks passed whilst I made inquiries in different quarters, to gather information on Invalidity Benefit. When I did write, I expressed surprise that he had replied to my letter, and by return of post. This was unlike earlier correspondence when it had been necessary for me to send him reminders to elicit replies. But on reflection, I continued, his reply was contemptible, because it dealt only with those parts of my letter which could be answered on a routine party political level. The remainder was ignored, just as he had refused to answer my earlier letters with little more than acknowledgement slips. I continued, that I did not want his sympathy, or any other empty pleasantries which were hypocritical, since he had refused to make any move to save other people from my wife's fate, or to change the law on suicide. I relegated my comments on Invalidity Benefit to a postscript. I wrote that the increase of 11½%

was well below the current rate of inflation standing at 16½%, and that the factors determining Government spending are complex and can be distorted by commitments to pay increases, for example. The question was, whether the National Health Service had improved in quality during the previous year.

Wilkins, my representative in Parliament, did not reply. The Department of Health and Social Security sent an acknowledgement card promising attention following my first letter, but they also did not communicate with me again.

* * *

In December, 1980, my neighbour, Alan, observing how the events of the past six months had increased our suffering and hopeless despair, suggested that I see a professional acquaintance of his who was a psychiatrist. Alan believed that his acquaintance held similar views to my own and might be able to help me. He did not specify whether such help might be of professional psychiatric form or that of a sympathetic person, with whom I could discuss my situation. Alan said that I had only to ring and introduce myself as his neighbour. I might not take to the man, he added, but in my current impasse this psychiatrist might 'open doors' for me.

I thanked Alan for showing concern for us and promised to think about his suggestion. My common sense told me that this proposal was ridiculous. I was much too experienced to believe that a visit to a practising psychiatrist could mitigate or solve the problems that I faced. Not only would the biological facts causing Mary's deterioration be untouched, but I believed as an axiomatic fact, that the pain I experienced daily because of the diminution of Mary's personality, was both normal and natural. So complete was my awareness of my emotional and intellectual needs, so strong and immediate my frustration when they were not satisfied, that it was impossible for me to believe that doors could open for either

119

of us. But, although my position was wretched, Mary's was desperate. Therefore, I had no right to dismiss any course without first exploring it. Feeling distinctly uneasy and embarrassed because of my insincerity, I telephoned him to arrange a meeting at his office.

A week later, at the appointed time, he ushered me in. It was not so much an office as a living room. This scenario increased my discomfort, for it made me feel like an intruder. I had no clear motive for being there, merely a vague need to glean any information or advice from what he said. I explained to him that my wife had Huntington's chorea and that she did not wish to let it take its course. I told him how we had become involved in the Ford/Smith case, and I briefly described our situation.

He responded in a quietly optimistic manner, and said that, for the moment, my wife's condition was not as bad as that of many people inflicted with serious diseases. She was mobile and essentially of sound mind. He advised me to "bone up" on the law, foreseeing that, in the future, if she carried out her intention to kill herself, I needed to be prepared for questioning or other action by the police.

Just when it seemed that this un-noteworthy interview would end inconsequentially, a dramatic change took place. Our conversation had turned to a discussion about Huntington's chorea, and, almost casually, I spoke of the need for sterilisation to curb it. To my surprise this drew a strong and uncompromising rebuttal from him. My response was equally strong, and within seconds a furious argument developed. Once more, I was face to face with the type of mentality that was the cause of the destruction of Mary's life and of mine, for here was a man who, being aware of the suffering caused by the disease, concluded that Mary's suicide would be the best option available to her. But, at the same time, he was opposed to taking action to eliminate the disease!

I remember that one of his arguments confused moral principle with expediency. He argued that, because we lived in a period when personal freedom and choice was thought to be normal and desirable, it was necessary to apply this ethos to families afflicted by the disease, in respect of their breeding habits.

I offered to pay a fee for the interview, but he said that, in the circumstances, it would not be necessary.

It was also in December that I was prevailed upon by a friend to speak to the Samaritans. She had received help following a broken marriage, and on a number of occasions she had urged me to go to them. For the same reasons as those stated above, I judged that I would be wasting my time. But similarly, I believed that I must not reject any avenue, no matter how unlikely it might seem to be.

I was introduced to Melanie, a large handsome woman, and she invited me to explain my problem. Melanie was a sympathetic person and a good listener. I talked for two hours, giving her a comprehensive account of the previous three years, and my assessment of them. I also ranged over the limited options that were open to me, and I spoke about my fears for the future. Finally, I asked for her opinion and for advice. They were metaphorical questions, and I knew this to be so even as I put them to her. It was really no more than a literary termination to my long and sometimes emotional narrative.

Melanie replied by saying that she had heard of Huntington's chorea, but until then, had known nothing about it. She said that my story was the most remarkable that she had ever heard. No, there was nothing she could advise me to do. The Samaritans never give advice, they only listen, and often the people who go to them for help gain insight into themselves as a consequence of talking about their problems. They might then take appropriate action to solve them. In my case, Melanie believed that I had analysed the situation so thoroughly, that even if the role of the Samaritans had been advisory, she would not have been able to make any suggestions. Mary and I faced problems that were intractable. Melanie invited me to call again. She was always available at that time.

Naturally, I never did. Nor did I ever again respond to any suggestions that I should look for public or private help. I did not know then, that in a short time, I would be the beneficiary of the only type of support that could possibly heal my wounded state, that this would thrust Mary further into hopeless despair, and that in the future that awaited me, I would have to pay for this support by ineradicable feelings of guilt.

* * *

Nineteen eighty, the third complete year of the calamity, was, apart from the shock of the diagnosis, the worst year we had experienced, but it ended with one event that removed a nagging concern. News came to us that Mary's father had died, and with his death the removal of any possibility that Mary could be disinherited.

Since October 1978, when she had been diagnosed, he had ignored her. He had not written, telephoned, or visited us. Through my sister-in-law, he knew what was happening. Due to this lack of contact, I will never know what his reactions were when he heard that his daughter Mary was going to deteriorate over a long period of time, just as he had witnessed her mother decline into physical decrepitude, insanity and death. Did he fear to communicate with us? Did he feel any guilt? Did he prefer to erase from his mind all thoughts of Mary, because she would remind him of all the painful years of his wife's deterioration?

When we heard the news, I detected faint tears in Mary's eyes. It was true that neither of us owed him anything, and his silence during the previous two years was unforgiveable, but I should have remained silent. I did not. I expressed satisfaction that, with his death, one problem was removed. Mary rapidly regained her stoical composure. Her grief may have been irrational, her father was not worthy of it, but in my state of chronic anger, she knew that a brief expression of sorrow might rouse me to direct yet another diatribe against her. Whilst expressing my satisfaction, I saw with pity the small defenceless child in Mary, but I could not relent. I could not allow my love and concern for her to weaken or supplant my own need to remain inviolate. I could not allow my own raging frustrations and my fear of the unknown future to stand naked and unjustified. Above all, I dared not allow Mary to become dependent upon me. I could never then escape from a situation that threatened to destroy me.

This little scene was only one amongst numerous others, when I gave pain to Mary during those years. The immediate causes varied, and some I have forgotten, but I am left with many regrets that I can never efface.

Chapter 9

I have mentioned above, how we joined a local Caledonian Society. Its functions became part of our round of activities and led to our taking up Scottish country dancing. It was a most unlikely activity for anyone afflicted with Huntington's chorea, and possibly Mary was unique in starting this pastime in her condition. At the time, I could not possibly foresee what it would lead to.

Throughout 1979 we regularly attended the Society's dance classes and they gave us considerable pleasure. Mary was in an early stage of the disease, and at first her physical disablement was not too marked. My own inaptitude for the figures matched hers, and in the early months she was marginally quicker at learning than I was. At the time, I wondered for how long she would be able to continue dancing, before the disease would stop her slow progress, and then reverse it.

For the sake of those readers who know nothing about Scottish country dancing, it is necessary to describe some features of it that are relevant to my story. Most Scottish country dancing had its origin in the English country dancing of the sixteenth century, but, since then, it had developed separately. Generally, it is much faster than the English form, and the figures and formations are more complex. To a Scottish country dancer, the English dancing seems, by comparison, to be both simple and tame. This comparison is also true when Scottish is compared to the American square-dancing. Another feature of Scottish country dancing is that it does not have a caller, except for certain informal occasions, such as teaching classes.

One important innovation made to English dancing, at least as early as the sixteenth century, and later taken to Scotland, was the progressive line dance. The great majority of Scottish country dances are of this type. Dancers pair off, man with woman, and form lines. The ladies make one line and their gentlemen partners opposite them, another. Each pair, or couple as they are termed, are then numbered off from the top of the lines into three, four, or five couple groups. Each group is called a 'set', and it performs the dance independently of the other 'sets'.

Within each set there is a progression. Thus, in the first sequence of a four couple dance, each sequence lasting for 24, 32, 40 or 48 bars of music, depending upon the particular dance, the first, second, and third couple will dance. During the second sequence, the first, third and fourth couples dance. The third sequence sees the twos, threes, and fours dancing, the fourth sequence the twos, fours, and ones dancing, and so on, until the end of the dance following the eighth sequence, when all four couples are back in their original order.

It will be seen then, that the progression adds a kaleidoscopic quality to the dance because of the constant change of positions, each one requiring different movements, and each one bringing dancers into constantly changing visual or tactile contact with the other seven.

In addition to the line dances there are a minority of square 'set' dances, in which men and women pair off into couples, and then form sets with four couples in each, in a north, south, east and west formation. Each of these sets will then dance independently of the others.

Scottish dancing, with its thousands of dances, of which at least eighteen will be danced in one evening, is as much a mental as a physical exercise. It is also a test of character, because of the stresses that its complexities of movement and its constant change of personalities impose upon dancers. It is not a pursuit that can be mastered quickly; it may take an individual several years. But, in spite of the difficulties peculiar to it, some degree of competence brings the reward of great pleasure to people who have the patience and persistence to continue.

Throughout 1979, Mary and I would go to dances, unable to manage more than a sprinkling that we had picked up at the weekly classes.

We would be taught some of those that were on forthcoming dance programmes, and in this manner we built up a small nucleus of dances, and a basic knowledge of the figures and formations common to many others. But, the normal steps used in Scottish country dancing were an insurmountable problem for Mary. Her lack of co-ordination made it impossible for her to do them. She would move with the characteristic stumbling motion, peculiar to victims of the disease.

To those people moving in Scottish country dance circles, it must have appeared that, at best, Mary, with her disabling disease, and I, possessing less aptitude than most beginners, would fade from the dance world as rapidly as we had appeared, and be quickly forgotten. Many of them probably looked upon our ingress as a little ridiculous; something of an intrusion.

Quite early in the year I discerned that there was a fundamental division amongst dancers. There were those who approached S.C.D. as an end in itself, and those who treated it as a means to provide fun. No doubt there were people amongst the former who disapproved of Mary, with her tripping gait, and rolling eyes as she strove to keep her balance, and, like a lead-weighted 'kelly' doll, swayed perilously without actually falling. I hope that, amongst the others, there were some who admired Mary's courage, unfailing good humour and sense of fun.

In the spring of 1979, we became acquainted with a man who was destined to become Mary's primary support, and to be the catalyst enabling us to break into a wider world of S.C.D. than we had enjoyed hitherto. Throughout the year we met John from time to time, but it was not until we started attending dance classes at Webley with him, that we became his friends.

In spite of the fun that we regularly enjoyed at Rusham, it was a backwater in S.C.D.. The range of dances taught was limited, and they did not include many newly devised dances that were popular in the London area. The class at Webley did practise these dances. Nevertheless, it became apparent to me as the months passed early in 1980, that the selfish behaviour that characterises certain dancers, was particularly rife in the Webley club. Beginners were not treated with patience, rather, in so far as they might be the cause of a dance falling into confusion, they were made to feel that they had committed a transgression, and were unwanted. Unlike Rusham, there was not a genuine change of partners for each dance. They changed, but always within their own cliques, the experienced dancers asking only the experienced dancers to dance. With the exception of John, other people never partnered Mary.

It was during this early part of 1980 that I came very close to stopping S.C.D. other than in Rusham. It appeared to me, at the time, to be a closed circuit from which we would always be excluded.

John has since told me that, when we were merely acquainted with him in 1979, he felt no more than pity when he was told what afflicted Mary. But, when he saw Mary regularly in 1980, he came to appreciate her qualities of good humour and stoical courage, and to dance with her out of choice, in preference to other ladies, because of the great pleasure that she gave him. It was at this time, that in addition to becoming our friend, John took us in hand to set us on our feet as Scottish country dancers. We also started going with him to classes, and Saturday evening dances.

Mary and I soon realised that John's knowledge of Scottish C.D. was greater than anyone we had met before. He had considerable knowledge of its figures and formations, its music and its history. Above all, John observed standards of polite deportment on the dance floor that, at first, I thought were a little old-fashioned. Later I came to recognise them as timeless, because of their underlying purpose of showing selfless consideration for other people.

John encouraged me to learn the figures and formations of dances at home, and not to be dependent upon teachers. He possessed a large collection of books and sheets of dances, and week by week he copied out instructions, with additional clarifying notes and diagrams, and gave them to me ahead of the evenings when they were included on dance programmes. I would transpose them into a diagrammatic form, and dance by dance, as the weeks and months passed, I built up a large collection.

Every week, in advance of the Saturday evening dances at St. Andrew's, I would assiduously learn all the dances on the programme, using my diagrams. My purpose was not only to be capable of getting myself through, but to be so conversant that I could also direct Mary. John often explained the unusual features of some dances, and we would walk through them under his direction. On Saturday afternoons, I would practise some of the more complicated movements with Mary, in preparation for the evening.

Other men never asked Mary to dance so, early in our friendship, John and I adopted a system of partnering her alternately. She was never left to sit out as a 'wallflower', so often the lot of beginners, who, for this reason, may turn away from S.C.D.. We were a disparate trio; John in his seventy first year, no longer a young man, myself a beginner, frequently referring to my pocket diagrams, and Mary, with all the classical symptoms of Huntington's chorea.

Throughout 1980, John, with unflagging enthusiasm drove us without respite and our dancing improved. He was convinced that the mental and physical exercise must be remedial for Mary. It was. It could not stop the relentless atrophy of her brain cells, but it became the only part of her life, and mine too, where we did have fun, and some purpose.

Mary's courage was unusual. Often she would line up for a dance hardly knowing the title, and having implicit faith that either John or I would direct her through it successfully. Very few ladies in the field of S.C.D. show the cool nerve, and readiness to trust their partners, that she did. She was able to get through many dances with little, or no prompting, from John or myself. In the less familiar ones, she showed an aptitude to follow our directions that could not be emulated by many experienced dancers, who were without her incapacitating disease.

When 1980 drew to a close, I realised with surprise that in the short space of one year we had progressed from being uncertain beginners, with no future in Scottish country dancing, to a position verging on confident mastery of the dance floor. With John's tireless efforts, my determination, and Mary's trust and courage, we had pulled ourselves up and achieved what should have been impossible. But there was, I believe, a factor which was more important than these qualities. It was John's unquestioning faith that, in spite of H.C., Mary would triumph.

The belief of some Christians that their religion has a spiritual monopoly, always surprises me. Of what value is faith in the Christian sense, when historically it has led to so much suffering, as with the massacre of the Albigensians or the wars of the Reformation? Of what value is it, too, in the selfish personal sense, of conferring salvation upon an individual? John was well informed about the nature of H.C., but he held to a simple, almost childlike belief, that Mary could, and should, enjoy the pleasure of Scottish country dancing. His temporal faith that tangibly eased Mary's suffering was much finer than any that Christians exhibit.

* * *

In addition to being John's dancing protégés, we became, as I have mentioned above, his warm friends. As the months passed, John developed into a father figure for Mary, and he was always patient with her. At all times, too, he tried to be bright and cheerful, even when we were hopelessly depressed. But there were tensions with John that were a direct result of my sense of outrage at the injustice that had been done to us. By early 1981, the succession of painful and bizarre events that the disease had brought hardened my intolerance, so that I demanded total agreement with my views, even from him. It required sensitive tact to avoid open conflict with me at that time.

During a brief discussion of the disease, John expressed the opinion that it was difficult to believe in sterilisation for affected families, because Mary would not then have been born to give so much care and support to people through her nursing career, nor would he and other people have been given so much pleasure by her company.

If Mary's disease had been less serious, and my emotions less explosive, I might have quietly reasoned with him, that if Mary had not been born she could never be missed. But I could not. I was no more capable of a calm response than is an animal that thrashes about when it is caught in a trap, so I sent John the inevitable letter.

I reminded him that he, as much as anyone, was aware of the extreme misery that H.C. brings, and of all the ramifications in its train that it had brought to us, giving as examples, the 'phone tapping and our estrangement from friends. In spite of this, he had decided against mandatory sterilisation, and thought that people should not be denied the pleasure given to them by Mary. I added, that it appeared he thought it preferable for Mary to endure years of suffering, before dying in a mental hospital, or when she was forced to take her own life. I finished by writing, that I could not accept this from him.

John replied at length, apologising for apparently giving the impression that he had made up his mind, and had dismissed my solution for H.C. as ill-founded. It was difficult for him to accept that Mary should never have been born, but maybe he should respect my opinion, since I had to live with the problem day after day.

John wrote that he had heard of people who believed that certain hereditary diseases should be controlled by sterilisation, and he dismissed this, but none of these diseases were as awful as Huntington's chorea.

So people, he believed, were against compulsory sterilisation because it would interfere with personal choice and be the beginning of a police state. It appeared that this was the opinion of my M.P., but he should have said so, honestly.

John added that he, personally, did not know what the answer was. Perhaps H.C., and no other disease, should be stopped by a sterilisation law. He could hardly be other than on my side, especially because the medical profession had failed to take a positive view, turning a blind eye.

He wrote that he was moved by my reasoned letters, with their intensity of feeling, and did not wish it to be thought that he had rejected my beliefs. He could not make up his mind on a question which, because of long experience, had only one solution in my eyes, but was perplexing to him.

John then quoted Kipling.

'If you can trust yourself when all men doubt you,
But make allowance for their doubting too'.

John ended his letter expressing doubts on whether life was worthwhile, but hoping that his companionship had meant as much to Mary and me, as ours had to him.

Following this letter I never discussed the subject again with him. His opinions were sincere and given unreservedly. Perhaps his most important observation was that he was not living in the situation day after day, as I was. People with the disease or at risk of it, and their families, are in a small minority, and their suffering does not occupy the minds of the majority of people, even when they have heard of H.C..

But, I could not agree that sterilisation legislation would lead to a police state. We already have many restraints that are enforced by the police in a modern society, and contagious diseases, for example, are strictly curbed because most people are at risk to them. By contrast, H.C. affects only a minority of people, and the unborn cannot exert any influence upon the breeding habits of affected families. But I have covered this ground before. The unavoidable conclusion is, that public health legislation is selfishly designed to benefit the majority.

Another friend from whom I demanded total agreement at that time, was Joan. She regularly took Mary for shopping outings in her car. They usually returned to our house for coffee, and on one occasion Joan and I had a very heated argument about H.C. and related matters. Mary remained silent throughout. After Joan had returned home, leaving me burning with rage, I drafted a letter to send to her.

I started by telling her that I did not wish her to come to my home again, because the argument had clarified the opinions she held about the disease. By saying that it was not my business to inform my nieces and nephew that they were at risk to the disease, and by comparing me with Nazis because of my assertion that all affected families should be sterilised, she expressed the two salient opinions that ensure the continuation of H.C..

I reminded her of the years of suffering behind us, and the much greater suffering that lay in the future. I found the opinions that had imposed this burden upon us, and wrecked our lives, intolerable, especially if they were held by a friend. I failed to understand how she could be such a hypocrite condoning the transmission of H.C., whilst purporting to be Mary's friend. I ended the draft by saying that I did not want her 'crumbs', and would now find it humiliating to accept them.

I showed it to Mary. She said little. She looked helpless and was withdrawn. She understood how I felt but, quietly added, that soon we would have no friends left. For her sake, knowing how consistently kind Joan had been, I decided not to send it, but in one respect it hardly mattered, because I would harbour resentment against Joan, and whenever we met this would show. The friendship could not last.

But I was wrong. Ten days later Joan wrote to me pleading for us to be friends, and expressing agreement with me regarding sterilisation. She explained that she had not made herself clear when we were arguing. She had not really been concerned about the issues raised, but was anxious that my opinions should not be the cause of so much unhappiness between Mary and me. Joan wrote that she loved us both, and pressed me not to relinquish all my activities. (This was a reference to my shedding of commitments with the R.S.P.C.A. and the Caledonian Society. I simply could not manage any but the most essential responsibilities, by that time).

Her letter, which was self-effacing and affectionate, enabled our friendship to continue. But her good-willed concern for me, whilst mollifying my particular anger with her caused by the argument, could not mitigate my general anger at the perverse opinions held by so many people around me. Neither could it assuage the violent emotions aroused in me by the effect of the disease upon Mary.

* * *

My annual leave year was nearing its end, and I was entitled to two more weeks. I felt that we could not waste them by remaining at home, and there was the problem that the irritation and stress that I would suffer from being constantly with Mary, could only exacerbate my already wild emotions, and intensify the interludes when I felt black despair. Mary, too, would inevitably suffer more in consequence. I decided that the best option would be a holiday in France. We would be completely away from our normal environment, but travelling in a familiar country that would not give us any more problems than if we remained in Britain.

In the following weeks I arranged the cross Channel ferries, the insurance, the itinerary, and a car-sleeper train. This would take us from Paris to

Toulouse, where we would begin our tour in the warmth of the south of France. In addition, I had to pack for Mary, and to organise the food that we would take. I managed to generate a little enthusiasm, because the preparations reminded me of happier times in the earlier years of our marriage, when we regularly travelled on the Continent.

During these preparations, I learned that the insurance company arranging our medical expenses cover required that all policy holders were fit to travel. I knew that Mary's condition might well be used as an excuse not to indemnify us, should she have to make a claim, so she made an appointment with our doctor to obtain a certificate confirming that she was fit. I guessed that he would charge a fee, and I advised Mary to refuse, since it was largely the irresponsibility of the medical profession that had led to her inheritance of the disease.

He did ask for the trifling sum of £1, but Mary refused to pay on the grounds that she was an ex-local nurse, not mentioning my reason why she should not.

Vaguely, I hoped that the holiday would turn out to be as enjoyable as the South African tour, but I was disappointed. In the intervening eighteen months Mary had deteriorated further, and her ineptitude put me in a state of constant irritation that the pleasures of the holiday could not allay. I found fault with everything that she did, and finally I insisted upon managing every detail of our day-to-day living.

We did have one noteworthy experience. We met a young Dutch couple, who were nearing the end of a year-long tour of Europe on bicycles. We sat with them one warm evening discussing travel, and then changed to personal matters. We told them that Mary had Huntington's chorea, and to our surprise they did not react by asking what it was.

"You have heard of this disease?" I queried.
"Oh yes" they replied, "We work in the field".

The husband was a mental nurse, his wife a psychiatric therapist. They expressed admiration for Mary and me for undertaking a foreign holiday and, they added, that really, Mary had very little chorea, a feature of her symptoms that I knew to be unusual.

We told them our story. It was obvious that they found it interesting, and they fully understood Mary's wish not to allow the disease to take its course. They took to heart the difficulties in obtaining drugs for her suicide because, following their return to Holland, they wrote giving an address in Switzerland where Mary might obtain drugs without any formalities. Presumably it was a black market source. I replied to them, but they did not answer my letter.

As the holiday came to an end, I knew that it would be our last one together. I could not face being alone with Mary again. Of more importance, I resolved to leave her. I could not endure life with her any longer. I decided to take a flat or bed-sitting room. I would not cut myself off entirely; I would telephone her every day, and I would be at the house several times every week to keep it in order. I could not envisage what my desertion would lead to, either for Mary, or in the reaction of friends. I was unable to think clearly about the future for either of us; I wanted only to escape. For Mary, there would be no escape from the disease. I could not save her, and I had reached a point where my support, although limited, was more than I could continue to give.

Having decided to leave, and being about to put it into effect, there came an event in my life that brought a dramatic change to it. Coming precisely at that time, it could be said to be yet another of the remarkable coincidences that occurred during these years. My decision to leave Mary was immediately put aside. In my changed circumstances, it became, for a time, irrelevant and unnecessary.

Chapter 10

I had met June a few months earlier at a Scottish country dance group which John, Mary and I regularly attended. I had seen her frequently, and she became one of a number of dancing acquaintances I had made at different venues. Immediately following the holiday, when we were brought alone together for the first time, we abruptly started a relationship that was born from mutual need. I did nothing to engineer it; I was taken by surprise, because of its sudden and unexpected start. From that moment, I felt the relief of being supported, even saved, by the constant, untrammelled, and intense love that she gave me. It exceeded any that I had received before. From the start of our relationship there was never any question or doubt about our future; it could only be together. I felt guilt, constant guilt, towards Mary, and it was heightened because I knew that it was she who needed the love that I was receiving.

I then began to lead a double life that was an entirely new experience. I knew that it was dishonourable and contemptible, but I could do nothing in the circumstances in which I was placed, to alter it. In the early months through April, May and June, I was very careful to give Mary no cause to suspect my infidelity, and I unrealistically hoped that her condition would make her less likely to detect it. Although it was not until summer that she openly accused me of consorting with a third party, I have since been told by a friend that she knew much earlier that a relationship existed. Mary never did learn who it was and, at a later date, when I did admit its existence, I led her to believe that it was with someone I had met through my work.

From April onwards I took to snatching what time I could with June, as circumstances permitted. Without fail, I would spend my Sundays with her, on the pretext of walking in the Chilterns. My dog was old and infirm, and it was quite impossible for him to walk more than a leisurely mile or two, so in the previous year I had often walked alone, whilst Mary remained at home with him. I believe that she encouraged me to do this, knowing that I needed to be away from her. When the relationship started, I merely had to increase the frequency of these outings, in order to be with June every Sunday. I knew, even as I left Mary Sunday after Sunday, that I was exploiting her loving concern for me.

During the previous summer, Mary and I occasionally spent Sundays together in the country, but in contrast to the great pleasure that it had given me in the past, I was incapable of enjoying these days in her company any longer. The state of tension that she produced in me was inimical to any pleasure for either of us.

I did manage to take her twice into the Chilterns during that summer of 1981, and both days were memorable. Each time we sat on a hillside overlooking the Turville Valley. The grasses around us stirred in the breeze, and the peacock butterflies clinging to the blue scabious slowly raised and lowered their wings as if in bliss. Wood-pigeons leisurely cooed in the beech woods and tousled poppies fluttered in the corn.

I watched Mary's face. It was months since we had been in France, and it had then been winter. It was more than a year since she had been in the English countryside in summer. Her eyes were open wide as she appreciatively took in the whole scene. She was like a child who is a little awestruck and silent, when given an expensive and unexpected present.

Throughout the years of her deterioration, Mary never lost her sensitivity to the natural world and to the arts. Amongst so many regrets that will always remain with me, I am bitterly sorry that I denied her so much pleasure that she was capable of enjoying.

It was ironical that it was my relationship with June that, for the moment, enabled me to remain with Mary. It also caused a marked change in my demeanour. I was less angry and not impelled to express it so often against Mary. It remained, but it was only aroused in response to particular incidents or statements made by other people.

In addition to the balm of her love, another calming influence at that time was June's immediate and intelligent grasp of the moral issues involved in the transmission of H.C.. Her readiness to listen to my analysis of the reasons for the selfish behaviour common to many affected families, and for the conspiracy of silence surrounding the disease, and her approval of my conclusions, was soothing to my inflamed mind. Only two friends had responded so unambiguously before, but both were amongst those who carefully stayed away from Mary and me.

June had not changed or modified her opinions protean-like to suit our relationship. Months earlier, at the beginning of our acquaintanceship, she had expressed surprise that people at risk continued to have children. "But why?" she had asked me. As the mother of two children herself, she found it puzzling that parents could perpetrate such a terrible legacy upon their children. She added to this that, should she have had children by a husband who later confessed that he was at risk to H.C., the marriage would, as a result, have broken down. She hoped that she would have got over such an admission where there were no children but, if there were, she believed that she could never forgive her husband. Additionally, her life would be ruined because of her frantic worry that the children might have inherited the causative gene.

I knew that deliberate withholding of information was widespread in Huntington families, and I had had some personal experience of it but, only a few months after the start of my relationship with June, my friend John came across a situation mirroring that which June had posed. His friend Ray was told that his daughter-in-law had confessed that she was at risk of H.C.. She already had two young children and she was in a third pregnancy. Ray and his son were ignorant about the disease, so John borrowed literature from me for them to read. John told me later, that Ray was very worried by this revelation of the future that might be awaiting his grandchildren. His daughter-in-law's pregnancy was aborted, but I never did learn whether the marriage survived. John has since told me that Ray never mentions the subject. Apparently, it is so painful to him, and he feels so helpless because he will probably be dead if, or when, the disease breaks out in· his grandchildren, that he prefers to ignore it.

One other significant change that June brought about in me, in spite of our relationship being secret and our meetings clandestine, was a sense of self-worth that the recent years had dissipated. It also produced a burning contempt for all those people who had been less than sympathetic to my situation. I reflected how safe their lives were, and how easy it was for them to give me advice from the security of their niches, which, although they might be uncomfortable, were incomparably preferable to the bleakness of my own exposed position.

* * *

One year had passed since Mary had made her positive move to get assistance for suicide from Leslie Ford and Martin Smith, and she was anxiously awaiting the publication of the Guide. Her life then, was forfeit, but learning that I had transferred my affections to another woman must have been devastating; the ultimate shame and humiliation for her. I do not know if the realisation that I had formed an extra-marital relationship, came suddenly to her. She was inclined to be taciturn, so she may not have expressed her suspicions immediately. Once she felt certain, the enormity of my betrayal may have been so frightening that weeks may have passed before she dared to seek confirmation by challenging me. When she did so, she delivered her question, "Do you have a girlfriend?" in a resentful, almost offhand manner, that was quite inappropriate for its gravity. I believe that she was too frightened of this new and emerging development, in her defenceless state, to react with healthy anger. The personality changes produced by the disease may also have muted her reaction.

To that first uncertain challenge, and to those that came in the weeks that followed, my answer was always a casual, "No". I qualified this sometimes to explain my absences when I was with June, by adding somewhat weakly, albeit truthfully, that I needed to be away from the situation at times. My vestiges of 'Boy Scout' honesty that caused me to despise myself for lying to her, were of less importance than my wish to spare her the pain of the truth. As the weeks passed, her challenges changed to become more forceful and even bitterly taunting. Perhaps, when she realised that what little remained of her world did not entirely collapse because of this new development, she was emboldened to express herself with more vigour. Finally, after three months, and in a fit of anger that was engendered by the feeling that her challenges were a threat to my relationship with June, I defiantly answered, "Yes, I do have a girlfriend, and I will not give her up".

In spite of my anger, I remembered to use the word 'girlfriend'. This was intended to convey the impression that the relationship was casual and not of special importance. I hoped that this might spare Mary some pain. Having made the admission, I continued in this vein whenever she upbraided me, or out of curiosity asked for details of my 'girlfriend'. But, this inadequate deference to her feelings could not ameliorate her pain and loss of hope, as I continued in my relationship with June.

* * *

In the previous July, Leslie Ford had been held for questioning by the police, and the Release office had been raided and documents taken away. The police investigations had finally led to Leslie and Martin Smith being charged with a string of offences under Section II of the Suicide Act of 1961, for assisting, and conspiring to assist suicides. There was also a technical charge of murder. Martin Smith had been refused bail, and since November he had been held in Brixton prison on remand. At different times since May, when the case first became public, it had been reported by the national and international media. This had led to debates and controversy about voluntary euthanasia in many parts of the world. The solicitors, defending Leslie and Martin Smith, had asked for full committal proceedings, and these were to be in mid-April.

Before going on the French holiday with Mary, I had been invited to call Leslie's solicitor to discuss the possibility of giving assistance in the defence. He was a youngish, unprepossessing man, who mentioned that this was one of the biggest cases he had handled. We talked for forty minutes, and arrived at the same conclusion that I had with Martin Smith's solicitor. If Mary gave evidence, it would be an interesting example of the dreadful position of so many sick people facing a degrading or a painful death, who had sought help from Leslie, but it would also be further proof of his legal guilt. I left when Mr. Moore said that he would contact me at a later date if necessary. It was frustrating to be unable to help, but not surprising.

The committal proceedings were due to take place at North London Magistrates' Court only ten days after our return from France. It had been agreed that supporters of the voluntary euthanasia movement would demonstrate with banners outside the courthouse, because it was anticipated that the press and television would be there in force. I would dearly have liked to go, but I was not able to get release from work. Mary and I agreed that she would go alone. Here, I thought, was an opportunity to publicise her case; it must not be wasted. None of my letters, some of which I have précised above, had drawn any significant or helpful response from public or private quarters. In direct appeals I had fared no better. Mr. Moore, for example, had suggested that I should contact Penny Tully and ask if she would do an article on H.C.. She had recently taken an interest in voluntary euthanasia and given it useful publicity.

I rang her, anticipating that at least she would be sympathetic to my case for eliminating H.C., especially because of its linkage, in Mary's case, to the voluntary euthanasia movement. I very briefly explained that my wife suffered from Huntington's chorea, and was searching for a way out through suicide.

"Why are you and your wife different from other people?" she demanded.

"We've been involved with the Ford/Smith case", I replied, "and this led to our 'phone being tapped during the police investigations".

"They got all their information from Martin Smith's diaries," she peremptorily rejoindered.

"Well", I continued, "I'm trying to draw attention to the need for Huntington's chorea to be eliminated by sterilising all people with it and at risk to it".

"You can't do that", she said heavily, "That's taking freedom of choice away from people".

Warming to her abrupt, near-rude manner, and recognising that there was not the slightest chance of having a sympathetic discussion with this virago, I replied quickly and aggressively asking, "What choice has my wife had?"

"That's different" she replied. "Why is it?" I demanded.

For a few seconds she was silent. "Well", she said, uncertainly, "I'll take your 'phone number and perhaps give you a ring." She never did, but I no longer considered her to be a fit person to write an article on the disease, so it hardly mattered.

The night before the committal proceedings, I made a poster for Mary to take. It measured 3' x 1'8", and it was stiffened at each end with bamboo canes. I wrote down three suitable captions and Mary chose one of them. I painted it on in bright red capital letters.

I HAVE HUNTINGTON'S CHOREA

YOU CONDONED MY BIRTH

THE LEAST YOU CAN DO IS TO GIVE ME VOLUNTARY EUTHANASIA

I rolled it in a plastic bag and gave Mary written directions for reaching North London Magistrates' Court, and she set off alone in the morning.

Throughout that day I waited impatiently for news, fretting because I could not be with her. It was early evening before she returned and told me about the day's events. She had reached the court in ample time, and, in company with other banner holding demonstrators, she had stood outside from 9.00 a.m..

From the start she had been the centre of attraction, because of the banner that she held. She had been photographed many times, and press reporters had taken her name and asked her questions. Against the many supporters of voluntary euthanasia she had seen only two people in opposition. They had been discomforted by the moral simplicity of her message, and had gone over to her to say, "We are sorry, we are sorry". At one point, a young and callow policeman nervously attempting to keep the pavement free for passers-by, had aggressively ordered her to move aside. At 10.00 a.m., with the start of the proceedings, she had gone inside the courtroom.

It was small and seats were limited, but other pro-euthanasia supporters had held a seat for her. She had been distressed to see Leslie in the dock. It was impossible for her to remember more than a fraction of the evidence that the Prosecutor had brought against Leslie and Martin Smith, but she had been shocked when the case of Mrs. Hilary Green was being presented. Mrs. Green's suicide had started the police investigations into Release, but it was particularly apposite as an example of the trap into which Mary would fall, if she delayed her own suicide for too long.

This lady had suffered from multiple sclerosis for fourteen years. She had steadily deteriorated, until at the age of sixty she was paralysed, except for limited use of one arm. Naturally, she was not only housebound but also confined to bed, and this had led to her developing many pressure sores. Twice in the past she had made unsuccessful suicide attempts. Desperately wanting to die, but being unable to affect her own release, she had managed to contact Leslie who had sent Martin Smith to her. Martin had duly assisted her suicide, but a post-mortem examination had revealed drugs, including alcohol, in her blood. Since there was no alcohol in the house, suspicions had been aroused.

Mary said that the most surprising statement came from Mrs. Green's husband, when he was giving evidence for the Crown. He had the gall, she said, to claim that he did not know that his wife wanted to die!

Mary said that the day had been stimulating. She had been the focus of attention for a short while, and many people had spoken to her. But it was not yet over. Although she had hardly noticed any television cameras, I guessed that they would have filmed the scenes outside the court.

We watched every news programme that evening, and they all gave coverage to the committal proceedings at the court. In each one Mary was clearly to be seen, selected from amongst other demonstrators, but each time, although she was holding her poster prominently, its message could not be read. When the filming was close it was too brief, and when it was sustained the poster was too far away to be seen by viewers.

Mary fared no better with the many photographs that were taken of her that day. None appeared in any newspaper, nor did any journalists ever contact her later. It is possible, that whilst the case was sub-judice, they preferred not to publish any articles about her, but that could not account for their disregard of her following the full trial, which took place later that year.

* * *

Shortly before the trial, I noticed that the Recorder was publishing extracts taken from a biography of a prominent politician. It was written by Dennis Lee, who was a journalist working for the paper. I glanced idly at it, but my attention sharpened when I read that this man's younger brother had suffered and died from H.C. years earlier.

I rang Dennis Lee the following day. He was sympathetic and prepared to discuss the politician's family and Huntington's chorea. His knowledge of the disease was sketchy, and he did not understand the hereditary transmission. When I explained it fully to him, concluding that the politician

144

must be at a one-in-two risk, he was unconvinced. He then dismissed the alternative possibility that the younger brother had been illegitimate, explaining that the family was not of the type to engage in extra-marital relationships. When I told him that I was trying to get publicity for my wife's case, he invited me to write to him.

I sent him a wad of literature on the disease and copies of my correspondence with James Wilkins. I enclosed a long covering letter, in which I suggested that the politician's family's reluctance to discuss the disease with him was probably because of the stigmatic hereditary factor. It was probable that the politician and his wife, did not have children for want of trying, as she had said to him, but because they feared he might pass on the disease. I wrote that, although the facts about H.C. were known to Government, the medical profession and afflicted families, I had not heard of anyone who was attempting to eliminate it. I mentioned the suffering experienced by my wife and myself, and wrote of our feeling of isolation, due to very few people acknowledging that the catastrophe that had befallen us, was not accidental. I asked him to imagine how he would feel, if he had a loved-one who had been put in a wheelchair for life by a drunken driver, and our society had no laws to curb driving whilst under the influence of alcohol, and did not consider it necessary to have any.
I told him that Mary intended to take her own life rather than wait to be committed to an institution, (the fate of the younger brother), and described everything that had happened to us following her telephone calls to Release, when the C.I.D. had intervened. I reminded him that the Ford/Smith trial would start soon, and Mary intended to stand outside the Central London Court with her poster, as she had done at North London Court. I ended by asking if he would try to publish her story, call for action to stop people from H.C. families breeding, and press for the introduction of voluntary euthanasia. I asked for the return of all the literature and copies, if he were not interested in helping.

Several weeks later, not having heard anything, I telephoned the Recorder office and spoke to him. He explained that he had passed everything on to another department for their attention. More weeks passed, and I telephoned again. This time I was told that they would not be doing an article and the literature would be returned to me. When it did not come, I wrote twice to Dennis Lee. He did not reply to either request for the return of my copies. I next telephoned the Editor twice, asking him to return them. They were never sent to me, nor was an apology made for their loss.

Once more, I was faced with what seemed like another example of the conspiracy of silence. This time it came from a newspaper. Dennis Lee's ignorance of H.C. had allowed him to mention the disease in his book and article, innocent of its implications for the politician. Could it be, that on reading my letter and the copies, he, and the editorial staff, had decided against publishing anything about Mary and H.C., for fear of drawing attention to the politician's connection with the disease?

* * *

The evidence presented at the committal proceedings made it clear that the Crown's case against Leslie and Martin Smith was very strong. I could see no hope of an acquittal for either of them, so in June I wrote to Mr. Moore.

I reminded him of our meeting earlier in the year, when we had agreed that evidence from Mary might damage the defence, but, I added, since the committal I had changed my opinion. I enclosed copies of literature about H.C., my letters to Wilkins and the Minister for Health, my letters to the London Borough of Hilton Social Services, and those that I sent to Fight.
I wrote that I hoped he would agree that the moral issues, which my letters raised, could be very useful in Leslie's defence, if properly presented in court. I reminded him that society commits the criminally insane into custodial institutions for life. Mandatory sterilisation would be a trivial imposition upon H.C. families compared with this, and with the disastrous

consequences for innocent people that follow from allowing them to breed freely. The letters from Wilkins and the Minister for Health were positive evidence of Authorities' refusal to take responsibility for people's health in respect of H.C.. This put Mary into a different category from other people, because she was not sick through accident or chance. I suggested, that if Mary and I were called as witnesses and Counsel asked the right questions, we could very effectively reveal society's irresponsibility in allowing her birth, and in continuing to allow the spread of H.C.. The inadequacy of society in not being prepared to guarantee that, in future, she would receive proper nursing-care, could also be emphasised. In contrast, Leslie did respond to her plight with humanity and courage, so our evidence would expose the moral abdication of society, and make a conviction of him blatantly hypocritical.

Mr. Moore did not respond with any enthusiasm to my letter. It was interesting, he said, and would be kept in mind. As a lawyer, I supposed his defence of Leslie would be confined to all the legal precedents and the procedures of a criminal court. The evidence that my letter urged him to use, would be suitable only as a last resort. Not that the law is a precise instrument that can be applied without prejudice. It is greatly modified by individual and collective opinions at any time.

* * *

Shortly after writing to Mr. Moore, Leslie contacted us to ask if Mary would be prepared to go on a television programme dealing with sickness and voluntary euthanasia. It was part of a series that was being produced by Northern Television.

We agreed to help, and early in July a representative of the company came to interview Mary and take photographs of her. I cannot remember precisely how Adrian Hartley conducted the interview. My memory is of a youngish man with energy and enthusiasm. He was kind enough to Mary, and also tactful, and it became immediately apparent, which I had anticipated, that his job was to vet people to determine if they were suitable to appear on television. Even before his arrival, I had half decided that her condition and her depressed state would make her unacceptable to them, so I was not surprised when she was turned down.

I had to write to Adrian Hartley to remind him to return literature on H.C. which I had loaned him but, unlike Dennis Lee, he promptly did so, with a cheerful covering letter and enclosing a colour photograph of Mary. I still have the photograph; it was her last.

* * *

The much publicised Guide, that had been delayed by an injunction placed upon it by a dissident member of the Release committee, was finally ready for distribution to Release members in June. Mary, who had been anxiously awaiting its publication ever since the police had intervened to frustrate her suicide, immediately sent off for a copy.

Two weeks later Leslie telephoned me to say that he had received her cheque, but frankly admitted that he was retaining her copy of the Guide because he feared that she would promptly use it for her suicide. With his trial due to take place in October, he was hoping that Mary would be available to witness for him.

From the moment that suspicion had fallen upon Leslie, he had denied being implicated in assisting suicides. He claimed, for example, that Martin Smith played the role of a counsellor to sick people and that he did not realise what was happening. It is my opinion that it would have been far better for him to have admitted the truth, and to depend upon the righteousness of his role in assisting intolerably ill people to die. His position then would have been morally unassailable. At worst, he could have been criticised for poor judgement. When he telephoned me it appeared that he placed more faith in this type of defence than his solicitor, Mr. Moore, but he was changing horses in mid-stream, and witnesses like Mary would be less effective than they might otherwise have been.

I promised Leslie that I would speak to Mary, and tell her that he needed her help at his trial. I would not mention anything concerning his anxiety that she might utilise the Guide for her own suicide. In retrospect, I can see that it could be interpreted that we were exploiting Mary. Nicholas needed her alive for his defence, and I wanted the publicity that her appearance would produce in order to advertise the injustice done to us.

* * *

I have written above about Mary's nephew's assertions that he was in the hands of Jesus, and his intention to have children, and my response to this. His wedding had been arranged for July, and we had received our invitations. We had heard nothing from Fred Chance in the fourteen months since I had spoken to him, but Mary and I agreed that we should contact him to ensure that he had spoken to Roy, and turned him away from his resolve to have children. This time, it was Mary who telephoned. What she told me afterwards was not reassuring.

Fred Chance said that Roy had been unforthcoming, refusing to give an assurance that he would not have children. Fred had added that he would not be officiating at the wedding, the ceremony would be conducted by another minister. Fred had admitted to Mary that he would not refuse to marry Roy, if the duty fell to him. He believed that, if both he and his colleague refused, Roy would go elsewhere to be wed.

I wrote to Fred Chance soon after to thank him for speaking to Roy but, I added, that we were disturbed because of Roy's unwillingness to be guided by him. I explained that we had discussed the problem with friends, and it had been agreed that if he pressed Roy too firmly, or refused to marry him, he might alienate him and lose any remaining influence. I enclosed literature on the disease in my letter, inviting him to read it, and to pass it on to his colleague. With this fresh reminder of the destructive nature of Huntington's chorea and the suffering that it causes, I wrote that I hoped it would give him renewed strength in his attempt to influence Roy. If he succeeded, then my wife's suffering and mine would not be entirely without value. I added a postscript, writing that, unless the position changed radically, we would not go to the wedding. We could not condone the possible result of such a union.

I also wrote to Roy's future parents-in-law, Mr. and Mrs. Stone. I had met them briefly, earlier that year, but I did not know how much they knew about H.C., or if they were aware that Roy was at a one-in-two risk of inheriting it.

I began by telling them that Mary had learned of the possibility that Roy would have children. I explained that I was not sure whether they knew that he was at risk to H.C., or if they fully understood the nature of the disease. I enclosed copies of literature about H.C., and copies of some of my letters, and I begged them to prevail upon Roy not to have children. I added that we would have been happy to go to the wedding and renew our acquaintanceship with them, but we could not condone a union that might lead to dreadful consequences. I hoped that they would be successful in persuading Roy and Catherine, in which case the suffering that had already been experienced by my wife and other members of her family, would not be repeated in yet another generation.

These letters were written on a Friday in June, and posted the following day. Mary, without consulting me, made the next move. I returned home on Sunday to find her looking unusually disturbed. She had telephoned Roy in the afternoon and made a direct appeal to him, a move that, in my emotional state, I had had the good sense not to try.

She had used every argument that she could remember, to dissuade him from having children. She had told him that, just as he had hated his own father, so his children would hate him. She reminded him that, unlike his father, he knew all the facts, and would be fully culpable should he have children. Roy, she said, was unbending, reiterating that he would have children if he chose to. Finally, in exasperation, she said she hoped he would get the disease, because he deserved to.

There had been an immediate sequel to this conversation, and it was this that had upset Mary most. Her niece Catrina, had come over, possibly with the intention of bringing some comfort to Mary, following her fruitless talk with Roy. But Catrina, in her inimitably wet manner, had tactlessly told Mary that the family were considering having Jim committed to the local mental hospital. Their intention was for him to stay there during the weekdays, and to be home at the weekends. Management of Jim at home was becoming increasingly difficult, as his deterioration proceeded.

Mary and I agreed that it would not be long before he was incarcerated permanently in hospital. She decided that, without delay, she must warn him of the family's intentions, and offer to help his suicide before it was too late.

It was an indication of Mary's courage and sterling personality that she could embark upon this course of assistance for her brother, whilst her own situation was little better than his. In retrospect, I am surprised that I raised no objection to a proposal that might well have led to a criminal charge under Section II of the Suicide Act, or even worse, a murder charge, being brought against her. Because she was suffering from a disease affecting her mind, one consequence could have been her own incarceration in an institution for the criminal insane, that is, Broadmoor. Even in retrospect, this possibility alarms me.

In the following week, when Jim was alone at home, she made her way to him. She warned him of the family's intentions, and she offered to assist his suicide. Mary said that Jim was completely unaware of what was proposed for him, and seemed incredulous that his family would do such a thing. He spoke vaguely about shooting himself before committal to an institution. She said that he looked awful, and was obviously beyond possessing the will to carry out his suicide, even with her assistance. He had left it too late.

This was to be the last time that she saw her brother. I have often tried to re-create the scene in my mind. Both of them would probably be chain-smoking, Jim grossly choreic, Mary twitching and her mouth pouting as she observed her brother. They would both have the vague and slurred speech characteristic of H.C., both ravaged by the same disease and parodies of each other.

The day following Mary's long talk with her nephew, I wrote again to Fred Chance. I explained that Roy's reaction to her had been even less promising than to him. She had been distressed by his attitude, which was a clear expression of the type of dishonesty that may have led to her own birth, and inescapable predicament, now that she had the disease. I described Catrina's visit, when she had told Mary that the family proposed to commit Jim to an institution, because he could be violent, and was becoming too difficult to manage at home. I gave Mary's reply, 'So that is how you are going to dispose of your father'. I wrote that he would not need me to explain to him the inconsistency of the Gordon family in condoning Roy's avowal that he would have children, whilst at the same time being unprepared to take responsibility for Jim, a victim of the disease. I added that this proposal to commit Jim to an institution, was seen by Mary as a pointer to her own future. I continued, that I had changed the opinions expressed in my previous letter to him, now that Mary had failed to influence her nephew. I believed instead, that, whilst Roy continued to be surrounded by a morally pusillanimous atmosphere, and the Gordon family continued, as Mary expressed it, 'to hide from reality', probably the worst would happen. I urged him and his colleague to refuse to marry Roy, and to say why, fearlessly. Their moral stand, I continued, might deter him from his course. Finally, I wrote that I could not think of another card to play. I found the Gordon family repugnant, and wished to go away and forget everything that had happened in recent

152

years. My marriage had really ended more than a year ago, although my wife continued to want, and to need me. I could not comprehend her despair and the intensity of her suffering.

The next move in this family drama, which effectively illustrates some reasons for the continuing transmission of the disease, was a letter from Mr. Stone, in reply to mine.

He agreed with my concern about H.C., but had faith in his daughter and Roy to do the right thing. His daughter, he wrote, had always said that she would not have children, but he knew no reason why she had to tell me. He would have been more impressed had I spoken directly to Roy and Catherine, rather than behind their backs to Fred Chance. He was surprised that the suicide rate for H.C. was not higher, because of people like me. He believed that I was obsessed with the disease because I was a crank, but I would stop my 'phone calls and letters, if I could see the damage that they did to his daughter. Before my meddling she and Roy had no thought of having children, and would not be bullied by me. He believed that Roy was entitled to happiness before he was stricken down, and it was his Christian and humanitarian duty to help him achieve this, and not to remind him that he had only twenty years left of normal life. Mr. Stone continued by expressing inability to understand the torment suffered by Roy, and added that Roy did not need letters from me, telling everyone of his condition. The wedding day had been turned into a nightmare for all concerned, by me. He wrote that he would hold me personally responsible, if anything happened to either Roy or Catherine. He ended by withdrawing the invitation to the wedding.

Two weeks later I replied to him, saying that he was unwilling to be honest and face reality. In August 1979, Roy's sisters told us that he intended to have children, and was in the hands of Jesus etc. and this was repeated to my wife in April, 1980. I added that he, Mr. Stone, could not plead ignorance, for Roy's assertions were mentioned in one of the copy letters that I had sent to him. If Roy's declarations had been no more than passing bravado, it would have been simple for him to assure Fred Chance and my wife that· he had no intention of having children. If he had never made the original assertions, or if he had later made it clear that he would never have children, I would not have written any letters. I continued, by disagreeing that people at risk should be left to make their own choice regarding children, which he implied in his letter. This opinion was the primary cause for the continuing transmission of the disease, and it had led to the stress that Roy suffered, and to my wife's present condition. I added that I had good reason to be obsessed with H.C., and that he would be, if his wife had the disease. It was for that reason that I could not trust myself to speak to Roy. Faced with his statements about having children, that is, by the attitude that had led to my life being wrecked, I could not remain calm. His daughter's forthcoming marriage had thrust a situation upon him that he was refusing to accept responsibly. H.C. would not go away, because its effect was delayed. I ended my letter by paraphrasing him. I wrote that, if Roy did have children, I would hold Mr. Stone responsible, for he was one of those people who were prepared to ignore Roy's statements, and therefore to condone his potentially wicked behaviour.

Mr. Stone did not reply, and neither did Fred Chance. Roy and Catherine were duly married in July. Fred Chance had agreed that Roy should not have children, but he knew that Roy might do so. He too, was hiding from reality.

There was a minor sequel. Later in the year Mary happened to meet one of Roy's Christian friends in a tea-shop. He had not been told why we were absent from the wedding, and appeared to know nothing about H.C.. She described the disease to him, and explained what would probably happen to her, as she deteriorated. She explained that Roy was at risk of it, and in spite of knowing this, he had affirmed he would have children. He had made it impossible for us to go to the wedding.

Chapter 11

I now come to an episode in my narrative, in which I cannot excuse my behaviour towards Mary entirely on the grounds of acute stress. My inadequate treatment of her during the past three years could not be justified, but I was powerless to control the passions that were aroused in me because of her steady deterioration, and by the indifference and the irresponsible opinions of the society in which we lived. When June told me that she must go away on holiday to a friend in Cornwall for two weeks, I believed that I could not endure her absence, and also remain at home with Mary, so I decided to go away. Instead of taking a holiday in Britain, which, whilst unfair to Mary, would I believe have met with her understanding, I chose to go abroad to The Faeroes.

At first she feigned resignation to my proposal, and this encouraged me to proceed with the preparations, but when she saw that I was serious, her mood changed, and I could see that she viewed my forthcoming holiday with near disbelief. It must have been the final proof to her that our marriage had ended. For many years we had travelled in Europe, Asia, Africa, America, sharing many experiences, but she was to be left behind when I went to The Faeroes, a place she had often said she would like to visit. It was the peak holiday month of August, and it seemed that everyone was away or preparing for a holiday. Mary, who most deserved any pleasures that life could afford, was excluded, and would never go on holiday again.

Before leaving, I wrote out a list of numbers for her to keep beside the telephone. They included those of friends, her doctor, and the dog's vet. Anxious, because I was leaving her alone, I wrote out instructions regarding the gas and electrical appliances, and the house security locks. Mary was slow and forgetful, but she had not reached the stage of needing explicit instructions. I remember her pained expression when I handed them to her. When I left by mini-cab for the airport she stood silently, blankly, in the doorway, one hand half raised in a gesture of farewell, and near to tears.

The holiday was doomed to be a failure. The weather was very bad. On most days there was rain, and it was heavy at times. I was racked by guilt, and also worried about what might be happening at home.

Following my return to Heathrow airport, I was very impatient to reach home. I feared that many calamities might have occurred whilst I was away. Notably, I thought of her suicide, or that the house may have burnt down.

Mary was out with the dog when I returned, but I could see that everything was in order. On her return we said little. John had taken her Scottish country dancing, and she had been invited to the homes of two or three friends. I asked her what it had been like whilst I was away. She was tense, and too frightened to show much emotion. She answered with one word, "Awful".

* * *

The starting date for the trial of Leslie and Martin Smith had been set for October. We had not heard anything from Mr. Moore, but Mary decided to go to the Central London Court and to stand outside with her poster on the opening day. The setting was very different from North London. It appeared from her description that, not only had she been the sole demonstrator on the entrance steps, but she had been totally ignored in the busy coming and going through the entrance doors. When Leslie arrived, he had been filmed by the waiting television crews, and Mary barely had time to greet him before he entered the building. Later, Mary had sat in the public gallery to watch, and once more she was distressed to see Leslie in the dock.

That evening we viewed all the television news programmes, but the coverage of the trial was even worse than at North London. Mary was filmed only for one very brief moment, and this was apparently by accident.

The first week of the trial slowly passed, drawing less publicity than the committal proceedings. The sensational details had already been revealed by the Prosecution at North London. There was very little left in the case for the media; just the pickings, and later there would be the verdict.

It is stating the obvious to say that the news-media does not exist primarily to inform people, but rather takes on a life of its own, with suitably modified interpretations and selections of events to suit its masters. This applies to 'quality' coverage, as well as 'popular'. The former differs from the latter only in the superficial details of style, and in reporting a different selection of events. Essentially, they are similar, for their reportage is like fashion that changes rapidly from day to day.

At the end of the week, Mary received a telegram from Leslie's solicitors asking her to appear at the Central London Court on the following Monday. We agreed that the trial was going so badly for Leslie that his solicitors appeared to be planning to fall back on a mitigating circumstances defence after all. Mary made her way to the City once more, and I slipped away from work, to be with her. But her journey was abortive. The defence, after all, did not call her. I believe that this was a mistake, for nothing could have been lost by her appearance. The evidence against the two defendants was so strong, that the revelation that they planned to assist a further suicide, Mary's, would have made no material difference. Her personal appearance, with her undiminished plea to be assisted to die before she was committed to an institution, would have been electrifying.

The trial ended with guilty verdicts on most counts. Martin Smith was found guilty on six, of assisting suicides, and Leslie on four counts of conspiring to assist suicides. To my surprise, Martin Smith, who had already been held in prison on bail for one year, was given a two year suspended sentence, and immediately released. The judge was severe with Leslie. He was sentenced to two and a half years' imprisonment. He appealed against verdict and sentence in the following January, and the sentence was reduced to one and a half years. He gained the full one third remission, serving a period of one year in prison.

I remember that Mary expressed feelings of guilt to me following the trial. She felt partly responsible for what had happened to Leslie. I reasoned with her, that the connection with him had not changed the course of events in any way.

* * *

With Leslie found guilty and imprisoned, the vague and unreal hope that Mary had clung to for the past year that he might, in spite of everything, assist her suicide, was irrevocably destroyed. Release had sent her a copy of the Guide several weeks before the trial, and she turned to that.

The Guide was explicit in its instructions, but all save one of the recommended methods required mechanical arrangements, to be used in conjunction with a drug that would act as a sedative. Mary shrank from the mechanical arrangements that were described and felt that she could only use the method that required the taking of a drug in sufficient quantity to be lethal. Her problem was that she did not possess any of the drugs that were listed.

I knew that it was my duty to assist her to carry out her suicide, but I did nothing. I was worried that if I made enquiries at random to obtain one of the listed lethal drugs, police investigations following her death might lead to my prosecution under Section II of the Suicide Act. Undoubtedly, we were on the Ford/Smith case files held by the police, but, in addition to this consideration, I could not bring myself to take an active role in bringing about her death.

No one wishes to die, it is irreversible, and the end of all significance for the individual, and eternity is a chilling concept. I believe the resistance that so many people have to voluntary euthanasia is based upon guilt. They cannot accept the finality of death, but they know that little or nothing is done for many of the incurably ill, who may in consequence prefer to die. To legislate for euthanasia is a public admission of the inadequacy of society. Some people prefer to avoid these issues, and to retain the existing haphazard situation, which causes so much suffering to countless numbers of people, especially the old.

I was not told until much later of the frequency, during the final months of 1981, that Mary asked her remaining friends for help and advice, regarding her intended suicide. One friend did pass her a substantial quantity of sedative, and then became frightened and stayed away. Another friend offered to be with her when the time came. Mary told me of an occasion, in November, when she spoke seriously to a third friend about her desperation and her wish to die. This friend, no doubt at a loss how to respond to such an uninhibited expression of despair, brushed it aside with a light response saying, "You have years to live". It was strictly true, but it could not console Mary. Its effect, and that of similar statements made by other people, only increased her isolation. She realised that she could not depend upon assistance from anyone, and would have to kill herself unaided.

* * *

As 1981 drew to a close, her lethargy increased and her reactions became slower. Her tendency, when she entered the house, to stand for long seconds in the doorway with a vacuous smile as she took in the scene, became worse. Often I would irritably exclaim, "Come in, then!" She also seemed to take longer to light her cigarettes. With growing anger, I would watch her incompetently fumble to get out a cigarette and put it to her lips. Then, long seconds would pass whilst she repeatedly flicked her lighter until it ignited, and next, most maddening of all, she would hold the burning lighter for more long seconds, having apparently forgotten why she lit it, before finally putting the flame shakily to the cigarette and inhaling. Often, very often, I would shout at her during this prolonged operation, "Light it then, light it!" Her face would go tense, except for her lips, which she would repeatedly purse with anxiety.

Mary occasionally mentioned incidents when she went shopping alone in the High Street. Once, her unsteady walk caused her to bump into another pedestrian with some force, and she had been verbally abused, and accused of being drunk. On another occasion she had gone into a pet shop with the dog, and he had started to eat out of an open sack of dog biscuits lying on the floor. Because of his great size and her own unsteadiness, she had difficulty in pulling him away, and not before the shopkeeper had angrily complained to her. The dog was in his fifteenth year and geriatric. He and Mary were a terrible sight whenever they set off together, both swaying and staggering from side to side.

In these months, she became even more careless when crossing roads. This was not a direct symptom of the damage done to her mind by the disease, but an expression of her wish to stop living. Joan took to gripping her arm whenever a road had to be crossed on their weekly shopping expeditions, frightened that she would be hit by a vehicle. Mary also continued to refuse to wear a seat belt in our car, in case it prevented her death in an accident.

* * *

Christmas came, but it did not bring us any peace. The pervasive air of pleasurable anticipation in the days leading up to the holiday, served only to irritate me, and the sentiments spoken by Christians were not only irrelevant, but offensive to us.

Mary gave me two or three presents, mumbling that they would probably be the last from her. Other than my own, and one from John, she had not been given any. Later that morning, whilst I was bathing, several members of the Gordon family called with presents. They did not enter the house. Mary told them that they would not be welcome. When I came downstairs, it was to find her fumbling over the wrappings with childlike expectancy. But, the pleasure she was experiencing was immediately crushed by my angry reaction, when I realised who had given them to us.

"They must be returned", I said, "We cannot accept presents from these people now, it would be condoning their moral turpitude!"

We had been invited to spend the day with Joan and her husband, but I refused to go. My emotions were turbulent and my thoughts disorganised. I would not be able to feign conviviality, so Mary went alone. In spite of being treated kindly, it was not a happy day without me.

Their daughter, Gill, drove Mary home late in the evening. She had turned to religion a year or two earlier, to become a 'born again' Christian. As she drove, she urged Mary to "Turn to Jesus, because only He can save you from Huntington". On being told this by Mary, I telephoned the Millers immediately, in spite of the late hour, intending to speak to Gill. It was Bryan who answered and, quite unfairly, he received a vicious diatribe from me, well laced with oaths, denouncing his daughter's stupidity. Christmas day ended, as it had started, with my uncompromising rejection of other people's misplaced philanthropy.

* * *

Throughout 1981 John, Mary and I, continued with the Scottish country dancing. It was the only part of my life with Mary in those years, to which I can look back with few personal regrets. Long before the year ended, Mary and I were able to manage any and every dance programme. I believe that Mary was unique.
I have never heard of anyone with H.C., not only taking up Scottish country dancing after diagnosis, but progressing as she did to master the pastime in concert with John and myself.

Mary's enthusiasm for dancing never flagged. She was always grateful to me when I walked her through new or difficult figures at home, in preparation for a dance. I fear that sometimes I became very impatient with her, as with a child who is slow to learn.

Although I have written above of increasing lethargy as 1981 drew to a close, it was significant that, following my tuition in the lounge or the garden, her demeanour would change radically. The lethargy would disappear entirely, and so would her vacuous expression. The other symptoms would lessen, and she would briskly do the household chores and dress for the dance. With another husband, capable of showing her the concern and interest at all times that I showed when teaching her dances, her life would have been less intolerable.

At the Saturday evening dances, John and I continued to partner Mary alternately but, in addition, one of our friends took to partnering her for at least one of the dances on a programme on every occasion. During 1981, another dancer, with whom we had no previous connections, also began to partner Mary. Both Winston and Rob gave her the respect and attention that helped to alleviate her painful awareness of being an outsider.

She was always very unselfish at the dances. If John was not with us, she would press me to ask other ladies to dance, in order to give me a change from constantly partnering her. If I did, inevitably, she would be left to sit out. John and I accepted that few men would feel capable of partnering Mary. She did need the occasional reminder and guiding hand, even in the popular and most familiar dances, but in the more complex ones it required total knowledge, a wide range of signals, and fierce concentration to direct her through them. There was, too, her appearance. She was attractive by any standards, and her personality was sweet and affectionate, but like all victims of H.C. she did look odd, and decidedly so on the dance floor.

But we did not accept, or find it easy to forgive, those dancers who avoided dancing in her set. They would not line up below her, and they would walk by a square set when they spotted her in it. Most cruel of all to Mary, there were times when a couple would leave the line above her after the numbering into sets had taken place, when they perceived that they would be with her. There would then have to be a recount, giving shameful embarrassment to Mary, who would be well aware of what had happened.

John and I could not find any excuse for this behaviour. The preparatory work that we put into the dancing ensured that, under our direction, Mary rarely disrupted a dance. This could not be said of many people, including some who avoided her. Instead of the praise and encouragement that were her due, social ostracism followed her to the dance floor.

In the closing months of the year I became increasingly sensitive to this cruelty. Not infrequently when Mary and I were at, or near the top of a line as sets were being formed, no one would join below us. We would stand waiting in exposed isolation as dancers scurried to join other lines, before they were obliged to join us when those lines were filled. This behaviour steadily diminished my own pleasure from the dancing, as my sense of social segregation amidst so much conviviality, increased. Taking Mary to dances began to feel like a duty. I did consider stopping, but not seriously; it was necessary to continue for Mary's sake.

This cruel and insensitive behaviour set off by Mary's condition, plus the wrongs done to us by our country, led us to ignore the customary closing 'ceremony' at dances, when 'Auld Lang Syne' was sung, and people stood for the national anthem. The bad behaviour went unchecked, and the gross wrongs were unacknowledged. It would be hypocritical to join in these ceremonies that symbolised good fellowship and patriotism, that we did not feel.

In the liberal metropolitan atmosphere of London, our mark of protest always passed unremarked, but at a dance in the rural backwater of Bucks, our recalcitrance had been carefully noted. At the next dance I attended, the M.C. had the temerity to threaten that, if I did not conform and stand during the national anthem, I would be banned from all dances in future. No doubt this man lacked much individuality, and compensated for this by identifying himself with the abstract ideas of Queen and country. He felt threatened when this source of strength, essential for his self-esteem, was ignored by us. Naturally, I did not comply, and as usual quietly changed from my dance shoes whilst the anthem was played. A dance committee member appealed to me afterwards to be, as he put it, reasonable.

I wrote a long letter to him a week later, explaining my position. He never replied. I have not been to a dance in Bucks since that date.

1981 was the International Year for the Disabled, but it had not afforded Mary the slightest benefit, nor had it led to any public understanding or concern for her terrible plight.

* * *

There were times when Mary was unable to suffer my absences, when I was with June, in silence. Her reproaches often drew noisy invective from me. I would angrily retort that I needed the support of my friend, and that without it I would have to leave. This was true, but it was very painful for Mary to be presented with her own inadequacy, and frightening to be threatened with desertion. Her bitterness once led her to threaten to change her will, in order to exclude me from her half share of the house, in favour of her nieces and nephew. But this was uncharacteristic, and she apologised to me immediately afterwards. On several occasions she sarcastically asked if, following her death, I intended to donate her clothes to a charity shop, and then invite my 'girl-friend' in to live with me. This would remind me of the intense humiliation that she felt. But the most incisive of her comments, because of its obvious truth, was her

164

prediction that, following her death, I would have ample leisure in which to regret my treatment of her.

Those moments, when the pain of my betrayal made her vindictive, were uncommon. Mary continued to love me, but because she could no longer express it directly, she did so by other means. At Christmas, for example, there had been the expensive presents she had bought me. She was always concerned for my health, and frequently remarked upon my loss of weight. She carefully put away a spare identity card photograph of me that I had brought home from work and had then discarded. Our relationship had been so badly damaged that she was forced into these indirect expressions of love. It was a mark of her dignity that she never vulgarly thrust herself upon me, in spite of the extremity of her despair and her need to be loved.

She was keenly aware of my own suffering, and frequently mentioned how sorry she was for all the trouble that she was giving me. She often recalled her childhood and her mother; all the tension and the many rows, adding that our lives had become a repetition of those years. Mary said that she had hated her mother, and understood why I could not tolerate her now that she had Huntington's chorea.

In the months following Christmas, judging that she did not have much longer to live, Mary would at times express regret that she would never again see some of the countries that we had visited together on our holidays. Occasionally, she spoke about going on one last big trip, but these vague notions were ephemeral. Without me she could not undertake a holiday abroad, and I did not respond to her musings.

The quality of our lives together declined even further. Merely to be with Mary irritated me intensely, and I constantly found fault with everything that she did. She was frightened and confused and this magnified her symptoms which, in turn, fed my own feverish intolerance. I despised myself, and inwardly wept for her, but I was powerless to change anything.

There were times when my fear that I would be trapped with her for long years into the future, made me callous and bereft of any sensitivity to her appalling predicament. Mary continued, for example, to buy clothes for herself, but more than once I chided her for this, saying that I could not believe that she intended to take her own life. I demanded to know for sure what her intentions were. I would say to her that I was not suggesting that she should do it but, if she would not, she must allow me to leave, for I could not continue to stay with her. I would be back constantly to maintain the house and garden and to watch over her welfare, but it would have to be from a distance.

Hollow words, true, but hollow. I knew that, without me, Mary would not want to continue living. But I could not go on living with her, it was reducing me to moral depravity. From the start of our relationship, June had made it clear that her flat could be my home whenever I chose. She wanted me out of a situation that she feared might lead to frightful consequences. I knew that in her direct and very feminine concern for me, she ignored other considerations.

But it was not really an impasse. The violence of my emotions frequently blinded me to the facts; that Mary had first made suicide her goal three years earlier, had seriously enlisted the help of Martin Smith and Leslie a year later, and she had anxiously awaited the distribution of the Guide since then. Many times throughout the past three years she had said, "I know I've got to get out, the only question is, when?"

Whenever I said to her that I must leave, she would beg me to wait until she had "Got out", as she tersely expressed it. "You know what will happen the moment that you leave", she would add, "the social services and other people will move in, and I wouldn't be able to do it then". She was very frightened at this possibility, but whenever I suggested that she had years to live, her reaction was even stronger. "No, no, I can't go through it all again", she would exclaim, and go into paroxysms of rage at my refusal to take her intended suicide seriously.

166

* * *

The information contained in the Guide gave Mary the knowledge to effect her own suicide, but, as I have written, she shrank from all methods save for the taking of a drug in sufficient quantity to be lethal. Failing to receive any suitable drugs from friends, Mary, in desperation, went to the Release central office early in the year to enlist their help. I advised her not to go, reminding her that Release would be closely watched by the police because of the Ford/Smith case, and they would not dare to give her the slightest practical help. Predictably, the Release staff were kind and gave her coffee, and pinned a Release badge on to her coat, but they were unable to do more.

There was only one move left to her in her search for a suitable drug. She was forced into asking her doctor for one on prescription. She chose an anti-depressant, which he could hardly refuse to prescribe for her, in view of her condition. She wrote down the name on a piece of paper and presented it to him, saying that one of her ex-colleagues had recommended it. On handing over the prescription, her doctor had said to her, "I hope that I can trust you", and Mary had found this, and going cap in hand and lying, humiliating.

She handed me the capsules to count, and to calculate if they were sufficient in number to reach the minimum quantity recommended in the Guide as 'probably lethal'. The damage done by the disease to her brain made it difficult for her to do the arithmetic. There were insufficient capsules. This meant another calculation to determine how many days, at the stated dosage, they would last before she could go for a second prescription without arousing suspicion. I did the necessary arithmetic and gave her the date.

It was done quietly and grimly. It could not be avoided. I knew, that for her sake and for mine, it was best that I did this for her. I could not conceive of another course, given the prognosis of the disease and the complete breakdown of our marriage. I was aware, too, that, if our marriage had not broken down, her position would have been very dangerous, for she might then continue until she had passed a point of no return, when she would be incapable of carrying out her suicide. It was unbearable to consider her incarceration in an institution. That would be the worst outcome of all.

I felt no guilt when I did those calculations, only nagging shame that this was to be my sole part in her suicide. I knew that my duty lay in giving her every assistance. I should have overcome my fear of the law, and my puritan reluctance to take an active part in her death. Had I done so, it might have atoned for my years of ill-treatment.

When the day that I had given Mary came, she made another appointment with her doctor, in order to obtain more of the anti-depressant. This time she saw a locum; a young querulous man, who seemed unwilling to give her any, but finally prescribed something like half the amount that she had obtained on the first prescription. Once again, Mary found it humiliating.

I raged when Mary described this second visit. How dare this locum show any reluctance to prescribe her a drug she needed, in order to alleviate the effects of a disease that his profession failed even to try to eliminate.

Once again, I did the arithmetic, adding together the two amounts and converting the sum into grams and milligrams. This time the total came to more than the recommended minimum. It was not greatly more, but I explained to Mary that her body weight was decidedly less than average, and the figure in the Guide was an estimate based upon average weight. She now had the means for self-immolation.

* * *

By March, Joan Miller was Mary's only friend who continued to call regularly and take her on shopping outings. Joan knew of Mary's intentions, and begged Mary not to tell her when she was going to do it. There was, too, a retired nursing colleague, who since Christmas, in response to Mary's deepening despair, had increased her occasional visits until they were frequent, if not regular. No other friends called. It was an open secret that Mary's suicide was imminent and, apparently, fear of any involvement with it caused the remaining two or three friends to stay away from her.

There was one other visitor at that time. The eighteen-year-old daughter of Claudia started calling to see Mary twice weekly, but her visits, although well-intended, were not entirely welcome. She was yet another of the young 'born again' Christians, and her mother had made it clear to Mary and me, that her daughter strongly opposed suicide, suspected what Mary's intentions were, and would not hesitate to frustrate them.

After several visits, Marina, seeing the hopeless nature of Mary's existence, offered, presumably with her parent's permission, to have Mary stay with them. She did not specify either a short period or a permanent arrangement. This hardly mattered, because although it was intended to be a practical means to assist Mary, it was hopelessly idealistic. It took no account of Mary's need to receive my love and to live in her familiar surroundings, and it ignored the prognosis. It was a sign of Mary's basic integrity and courage, that she rejected this offer. At a later date, Marina reminded me of it, but I believe that she did so to exculpate herself from any guilt for that which had taken place, rather than to pass blame on to me, because it was Mary's decision to refuse the offer, not mine.

* * *

My leave year ended in March, but I had three weeks to take, and two of these had to be used before the end of the month. I could not go away on holiday with Mary; to be constantly together was impossible, and I could not repeat my shameful blunder of the previous August when I had deserted her for two weeks. To remain at home would place us together for longer periods, but it offered the least difficult alternative.

Mary pressed me not to waste the leave, but to go away. She said that she quite understood I could not take her with me. But above all these considerations, I knew that I must be on hand because she would not delay her suicide much longer.

The leave was as difficult as I had anticipated. I filled the days by doing minor repairs to the house. I remember that on the first day I broke off to drive Mary for her weekly appointment with a hairdresser. I told her to ring when she came out and I would collect her, but because I had grumbled when taking her, she returned by bus. She always gave me as little trouble as possible.

* * *

On the first Saturday of my leave, we went to the Scottish Club Ball at Chester Hall. John was not able to go with us, so I partnered Mary alone. It was a joyless evening. Never before had Mary been so difficult to guide through the dances. Since Christmas the progression of the disease and the extremity of her despair had led to a marked diminution in her ability, and that night she seemed to take another downward lurch. With grim determination I directed her through dance after dance. We were an island of tragedy amidst a sea of smiling faces. The indifference shown to us by the other dancers was only broken by those who avoided us when sets were formed. When two dancers whom I respected did this, I was, for the first time ever, stung into action. During the interval I challenged them politely, but firmly. I managed to show unusual restraint. I asked why they had avoided us, and stated that it was not Mary's fault that she had H.C., and that dancing was her sole remaining pleasure. I added that, the disease being hereditary, it was the collective responsibility of people to support her, because society had given it to her by condoning her birth.

After her death, one dancer apologised to me for the general lack of help given to Mary. He excused himself by saying that he had believed she was a bad dancer. Had he known she had Huntington's chorea, he would have given us assistance. I thanked him, but silently reflected that, whatever the reason for an individual's inadequacy, be it age, or incompetence, or disability, they should be treated with consideration. His sentiments came too late for Mary, because she would never dance again.

* * *

Following this weekend, we talked about her intended suicide. Mary was now broken, and when she spoke it was usually with an ironical and bitter tone. She was not only crushed and diminished by the disease and the years of relentless anger from me, but she had become thin and her face was pale and drawn. Her once cheerful smile had gone forever. She suggested either the next weekend or the following one, which was Easter. "Make it the next weekend", I replied. I was frightened, but I was even more frightened that she might not do it. I could not bear the delay of a further week. "You must go away for the weekend and take the dog," she said. "I will cancel the Sunday paper and the milk".

I saw June on Wednesday and told her what Mary proposed doing. She found it unreal. I said that I would go to an hotel Saturday evening, but she wanted me to stay with her. I explained that police investigations would follow. For myself it was immaterial, but I saw no need for her name to be mentioned if the C.I.D. demanded to know where I had been. After a discussion she prevailed upon me to sleep at her flat.

There remained Thursday and Friday. Mary had two more days of life left, but this was merely an idea in part of my mind. It did not infuse my whole being as an important truth does. Perhaps she would not go through with it; surely, I thought, she could not be serious. She had made no grand gesture, merely a quiet statement that this weekend she would do it. "I know I have to", she had said, "you can't take any more from me."

Thursday was warm and sunny. I could think of nothing better than an outing to the country. As we were preparing to leave, Mary accidentally trod on a cement drain surround that was still wet from my work of the previous day. I exploded with anger, and meanly threatened not to go. The disease was fast destroying me, also. Even the knowledge of her impending suicide, could not moderate my extreme anger at her slightest misdemeanour. I repaired the damage, but her vestigial footprint remains, not only as a sentimental token of her physical presence, but also a painful reminder of my intolerance.

We spent the day at Summer Heath Common in one of the loveliest parts of the Chilterns. It was here that we had camped and picnicked numerous times in past years. Beside the grove of larch, the beech wood and the summer ferns, we had enjoyed some of our happiest times together. It was from here that we had set off on walks to Ibstone, Nettlebed, Russell's Water, and Christmas Common.

In the afternoon our friend Derek, a local man, happened to pass by. At times in the past we had joined him in his secluded cabin to yarn and to drink whisky, Derek's little Jack Russell terrier on his lap, and our dogs lying in front of the wood fire. He sat with us for a time, but conversation was desultory. Derek was always cheerful, but he was unable to break through our despair. He knew Mary had H.C., and he understood the situation but, it was not until I walked with him for a short distance when he left us and intimated that she contemplated suicide, that it may have occurred to him that he might never see her again.

Later in the day, I suggested that she walk to Ibstone along the footpaths crossing the Turville valley. I would take the car round the country lanes and meet her at the other side. I knew that it would be her last chance to cross Turville Heath, past the grey stones of the Grange, and to see the horses in the nearby meadow, which always came trotting over when they spotted the dogs, to frisk and curvet round us.

Mary brightened at my suggestion and set off briskly and purposefully.

She hardly seemed to sway or stagger. I had long forgotten how she had walked before being stricken with the disease, and as she receded I thought, surely she was too vitally alive to destroy herself. It was madness whilst she was so physically capable and so alert. For a brief moment the sickening weight upon me lifted. It was not too late to stop her suicide, something could be saved from the sordid mess. I could confiscate the drug she had obtained, just as I had taken drugs off her two years earlier when she had threatened to kill herself.

This fleeting moment of optimism rapidly dissolved as my good sense returned. There was not the slightest possibility that I could support Mary in the future, and without me she could not go on living. To seek temporary relief for myself by stopping the impending disaster, would be cowardly and ultimately very cruel to Mary. She was steeling herself to do it, so I must stand by her for this final act. My wretched inadequacy over the years had helped bring her to it; I could not fail her now.

The outburst in the morning was the last occasion on which Mary was to suffer my anger. I remained calm, and a little in awe of her during the following forty-eight hours.

The following day was again sunny, and we drove out once more to the Chilterns. We sat on a hillside below Ibstone, amidst the withered stalks of the previous summer's ragwort. The primroses were rising out of the winter-seared earth; bright yellow flowers with mint green leaves. Below us in a ploughed field streaked with grey chalk, pieces of flint glittered in the strong sunlight. Beyond the field was a broad belt of beech trees, leafless and dark, the ground beneath them covered with the tea-red leaves from last summer.

Mary was quietly appreciative of the scene before us. The dog in his dotage, slept. I wrote my weekly letter to Leslie in prison and expressed thanks to him for his response to Mary two years ago. I judged that I would not be writing again for many weeks.

The sun steadily sank and disappeared behind the trees of Turville Heath. The light dimmed and the colours slowly faded. The air felt chill. Before it was dark I said, "We'd better go now". One final look round, and then, for the last time, we walked in silence, up the dark bridleway to the car.

Back at home Mary prepared a meal which we ate without a word. It was late, but I suggested listening to music outside. For two years or more I had not been able to bear her beside me in that most intimate of experiences. Her mere proximity had felt like an intrusion that embarrassed me. She had been deprived of the pleasure of music, because she always declined to listen alone, even when I pressed her to.

She left the choice to me. First a Schubert piano sonata, intimate and discursive, and finally the four Impromptus, the ultimate expression of transcendent escape.

'These drops of sound, spaced with precision,
With delicate power dissolve my will,
Disarming conflict and my thoughts,
Timeless, but bringing past to present.

This magic beauty that destroys,
This anaesthetic giving pain,
Taking me to the mindless void
That always is my destination.'

* * *

It was late when I woke Saturday morning. I had lain for hours before going off to sleep. I saw bright sunlight entering through chinks between the curtains, and then I remembered which day it was, and felt sickening despair at what lay ahead.

We ate breakfast slowly, then cleared the dishes from the table and washed them in silence. I was vaguely aware that I would soon be with June, but it brought me no anticipatory relief. I carefully locked and bolted the back door and, in a low strangulated voice, told her not to open the doors to anyone. I did not have to leave immediately. I sat at the kitchen table and Mary stood leaning with her back to the window, just as she had when I experienced the beatific vision. She had not dressed, she had no day to dress for, and she remained in her dressing gown. She was silent, expressionless, and a little remote. "Don't worry if you don't do it", I said, my voice faltering and my eyes blinded by tears, "We'll have to think of something else". Dazed and uncomprehending, I drove the car out of the garage and into the drive and then returned for the dog. "I'll put him in the car now", I said.

Mary knelt over him holding her head against his, and running her hands over his body, the mutilated one like a small half clenched fist, whilst he, innocent and unknowing, gently nudged her face with his muzzle.

I led him out to the car and returned to Mary. One last embrace and final protestations of love; she calm, tearless, slightly bitter, me dazed and crying silently.

One final word from Mary, "There is no point in my doing it if you are going to be like this".

I had driven half out of the drive, before I realised that I was still in slippers. Back again, and into the kitchen to collect my shoes. Mary was standing where I had left her, the sunlight all round her head.

"I love you", were my final words, and she nodded very slightly and half raised her hand in farewell.

* * *

I cannot remember the journey as I fled to June, She had not seen or heard from me since Wednesday. She looked frightened when I recounted the last two days. I do not believe that she had taken Mary's suicide seriously. The circumstances had drawn reactions from Mary and me that were entirely outside her experience of life.

During the weekend that followed she did her best for me. I was fed and she gave me her love, but she could hardly alleviate my anxiety, my fear and my remorse. As the hours slowly passed, I desperately wanted to know what was happening at home. In my agitated state remaining indoors throughout the weekend was impossible. The flat felt claustrophobic, so as much for my sake as for the dog's, we went out to the country on both afternoons. On Sunday especially, I badly wanted to turn off the road and go to Mary. I had explored every circumstance in my mind, and in all but one she would need me with her.

After two long days and a sleepless night between, Sunday evening finally came. It was time to return home. By then I was frightened, because of what I might find. But it could not be avoided. I left June soon after eight. She was also frightened, but she told me I must not forget that, whatever happened, she loved me and that I was not alone.

Chapter 12

It is true, that many times in the years following Mary's diagnosis I had been uneasy when returning, not knowing what might have happened in my absence, but that Sunday evening was different. Feverishly impatient, my stomach feeling hollow, my breath jerky, I drove up to the house. It was in darkness! She had done it! She had done it! Hurriedly I parked the car, slammed shut the door, ran across the lawn, fumbled with the key, and pushed in the door. Blackness within, but then, horror, out of the void came moans; she was still alive!

I ran upstairs. The rear bedroom - the moans came from the rear bedroom. I pushed open the door and my hand swept down on the light switch. Bright, clear light, showed every detail of the room. Three, four, perhaps five seconds I stood there in the doorway near the foot of the bed, registering the scene. What had gone wrong? Why? Why?

Mary was lying on the floor on her back, wedged between the bed and the wall where she had fallen. Her head was against the skirting running behind the top of the bed. The bedside cabinet normally against the skirting had worked down to near the foot of the bed, to just below her feet. She was clothed just as I had left her, thirty one hours earlier. Pants, and a nightdress and dressing gown which had worked their way up to her shoulders. She was moaning and twitching, and her eyes were wide open and unseeing, as her head rolled from side to side. Her knees and elbows were raw. One toe was grazed and cut. She was bruised along her shins and forearms. Her right upper lip was swollen, and her mouth and tongue were as if burnt. Her blood stained the carpet and was smeared on the wall beside her. There were two empty medicine bottles, and capsules were scattered about.

I was appalled and overwhelmed by what I saw. I did not pause to think, but even had I done so my course would have been the same. Without hesitation, I ran to my neighbour Alan for assistance. As he opened the door in response to my hammering I almost fell into his hall.

"Mary has tried to kill herself," I exclaimed, "I knew she was going to do it, but I didn't help her".

He led me to a chair. His wife Dierdre appeared briefly, and then she and Megan, a nurse living next door, ran round to Mary. Meanwhile, Alan was telephoning for an ambulance. I was in a wildly agitated state and hardly able to sit still whilst waiting the few minutes for it to arrive.

When it did, Alan and I followed the crew up to the bedroom. Dierdre and Megan had lifted Mary on to the bed and were comforting her, and Megan's husband David, was collecting the scattered capsules and placing them in one of the bottles. It was as the crew placed their resuscitation equipment down, that the significance of the scene broke through my near frenetic state. It was then that I realised that from the instant Alan had telephoned for an ambulance, Mary was on a conveyor, in which everyone would do the conventional things expected of them, devoid of all personal moral responsibility. I reacted immediately, and started to insist that Mary must not be revived.

I pointed to the equipment saying, "What's that for?" and not waiting for an answer quickly followed it with, "You're not going to revive her", my voice rising to a shout.

I then gripped the arms of both the ambulance crew to emphasise my determination, and as they turned to me with startled faces I launched into a rapid explanation about Mary's condition and her wish to die. But it became obvious, that both they and my neighbours were against me and intended to get Mary to hospital for treatment. Alan said that it was no time for me to raise moral objections, and I angrily replied that it was precisely now that people must start to be responsible and not revive Mary.

The ambulance crew I could excuse. They had never seen or heard of Mary or myself before, and it is probable that they knew little or nothing about H.C.. This was not true of the others; they knew much of our story and understood the nature of the disease. They had had years in which to observe Mary's deterioration, but they had never offered to help her. That evening they wanted to thwart her suicide. Alan, especially, surprised me at the time. It was he who had advised us to contact the Euthanasia Society three years earlier, but at this juncture he was prominent in pressing me to allow Mary to be medicated. His change of position may have been due to fear that, as a highly placed social worker, he would put himself at professional risk to be associated, in any way, with advocacy of suicide.

At a later date, David apologised to me for what had happened, and for several months Megan was so sensitive that she was ashamed to look at me or to speak. Dierdre, too, was uneasy in my presence, but I was not clear precisely why.

The impasse produced by my refusal to allow Mary to be taken to hospital, was only broken when our doctor arrived.

I never did learn who telephoned him. He looked a little embarrassed and asked to speak to me privately. We went into the lounge, and he encouraged me to enlarge upon the course of our lives since the inception of the disease. Even then, in my state of extreme excitement, it occurred to me that any doctor with a patient suffering from H.C., should have taken an active interest in her welfare long ago. As I paced back and forth, wildly damning the society that had done so much harm to us and caused so much suffering, he expressed surprise that I had been able to cope with my work. But his solicitous concern was no more than a subterfuge to keep me engaged whilst, unknown to me, Mary was taken out to the ambulance and driven away with Dierdre and Megan.

The moment I realised that I had been fooled by a cheap device, I hustled

179

everyone out of the house and, with the warnings of Alan and Williams that I was not in a fit state to drive, I sped off after the ambulance.

* * *

I have no clear recollection of the three miles drive to the Hospital other than my desperate fear that I would be too late to stop them treating her and bringing her back into the nightmare. I drove straight to the accident building, left the car at the nearest available space, and ran in through the entrance. Seeing Dierdre and Megan in the vestibule, I called out, "Where is she?" and they indicated the direction. Round a corner and along a corridor, and there she was in a clinic to the side, on a high wheeled bed, moaning and twisting.

As I reached her side I called out that she was not to be treated, and several people turned surprised faces to me. I was in a highly emotional state and made no attempt to hide it. I argued vociferously and ferociously with anyone who came near. At one stage, I gripped a nursing sister's arm and poured out Mary's story; she had H.C., and to avoid a terrible end she had rationally and bravely tried to take her own life. To revive her, and take her back into the nightmare of H.C. would be grossly cruel. I argued philosophically with a young Chinese doctor, who said that he must think of his job, and that he was obliged to medicate my wife. In reply I cited Eichmann, who, at his trial, had defended himself by claiming that he was only carrying out orders. I snarled at an English doctor that, "members of your bloody profession deliberately maintain a conspiracy of silence around the disease and do not warn people that they are at risk from it and must not have children." He replied, "I always keep my patients informed." I viciously said, "Then next time you go to a meeting of the British Medical Association, you raise the question and get something done!"

Uniformed police appeared, young and confident. One looked a little embarrassed when I once more poured out my story to them. The other

180

said that I must allow the doctors to treat Mary. I had parked the car on a double yellow line and they wanted me to move it. I feared that it was another ploy to take me away from Mary. More police came, and one with a beard contemptuously asked why I had called an ambulance.

"I didn't, a neighbour did", I replied.

This man obviously grasped the moral issue involved, but clearly despised me in my hysterical condition for not handling the situation better. There were then four policemen, and it dimly occurred to me, that calling so many to the hospital could only mean that, at a word from the hospital authorities, they would remove me by force.

The next person to approach me introduced himself as, "Bird, C.I.D.." He asked me to accompany him outside into the corridor. He walked before me, his head bent slightly forward. He was smooth and quite undistinguished. He spoke in a confidential manner, asking where I had been that day.

"In the Chilterns with a friend".

"Had anyone called?"

"How should I know? I wasn't there".

He then asked a question as a statement of fact. "You and your wife are members of Release?"

"Yes", I replied.

Then quickly he followed it with, "How did you know your wife had attempted suicide?"

"I found her moaning, with capsules scattered around; she had taken an overdose".

Without waiting for another question, I continued with the accusation, "Your 'mates' in the C.I.D. tapped our 'phone. If they'd not interfered, my wife would be dead and beyond suffering long ago. "

Bird denied personal involvement saying, "I didn't".

When I said that I should have been by my wife's side when she did it, but if I had been, no doubt he would put a charge on me, he did not reply. The interview ended when he, like everyone else, told me to allow my wife to be treated. He then padded silently away.

Whilst all this was taking place, or rather, between the many exchanges with different people, I was bending over Mary holding her hand and weeping freely. On the other side was a young nurse holding Mary's other hand and listening sympathetically to me as I spasmodically told her our story. I will never know her name but in all that company she alone, tacitly supported my stand. At times, between her incoherent babbling, Mary's mind would clear, and she would put her arms around my neck and kiss me, saying that she loved me.

The next person to appear was my neighbour Alan. He had telephoned June for me, and he quietly tried to persuade me to go to her, and to "Leave Mary to the medical staff, they know what to do". He added that, whilst I might have considerable energy, I could not continue without sleep.

To these blandishments I replied, "You won't subvert my moral responsibility to Mary, I must stay to ensure that she is not given more than nursing care".

At one stage it was suggested that Mary would live for only three more hours unless she was treated, but I never wavered from my resolve. I was appalled at the thought of her surviving. I asked the English doctor, whose name I later learned to be Hickman, if Mary might suffer additional brain damage from the drug if she survived untreated. This possibility was the only nagging doubt in my mind. He said, "No", so I firmly reiterated that she must not be touched. This knowledge gave me total confidence in my stand, because I knew that nothing could be lost from it.

I cannot remember by whom, but I was asked if my wife had a Release Declaration in her doctor's wallet, stating that she did not wish to be revived etc..

"Yes", I replied, "there is one".

Vaguely, I remembered that I had mentioned this Release Declaration to someone hours earlier, but a doctor had said that it had no legal validity. Soon after answering this question, I was told that it had been decided that my wife would not be treated, and would be given nursing care only.

This brought me immediate relief. I had passed another hurdle. I had only to wait for the drug to take its intended course. I could not think clearly of what lay beyond the next few hours. Suddenly I felt very weary. I reflected that had I pressed them earlier to ask Dr Williams to produce the 'Declaration', the weight of opinion may have shifted away from treating Mary soon after she was taken to hospital. I would then have been spared the extreme anxiety of those hours, and the lengthy public exposure of my near frenetic state.

Several days later my neighbour Alan suggested that the hospital authorities probably realised that, if they treated Mary against her wishes and she had survived with mental or physical damage, it would be open for me to sue them.

Following the decision not to treat her, I was told that an Inspector Flowers would like to speak with me. I went outside into the corridor where he was waiting. He was a gentleman. He quietly apologised, but explained that he had to obtain a few details from me for the inquest. Mary was not dead, but the sudden agreement that she would not be treated, followed by Inspector Flowers's quiet acceptance of her inevitable death was chilling, and it thrust all the responsibility for her future back into my hands.

* * *

From that moment, I never left Mary's side. The nurse took her blood pressure, and Hickman drew a very large sample of her blood. Taking it from a vein gave Mary distress, and she flinched whilst it was being done, trying to draw her thin and vulnerable arm back. I tartly asked if the sample was necessary, to which he replied that it was. I continued by asking if he was taking it for legal reasons. "Partly", was his curt reply.

Soon afterwards, at midnight, still moaning and twitching, Mary was wheeled out of the accident department and into a ward. The night nurses placed screens round her bed and I helped to put up cot sides, but since their locking devices were ineffectual they swung outwards under very little pressure. For the next thirty-six hours this was to be a constant problem, because Mary could not be left unattended even for short periods, in case she fell out of the bed.

I drew up a chair alongside, leaned against the cot sides and held her arm. She was never still or silent. Her limbs constantly jerked and she babbled incoherently. She seemed less aware of her surroundings than when she had been in the accident department, but if she was left alone, she usually attempted to climb out of bed, and she had to be restrained and comforted. Occasionally, if she quietened a little, I sat with the night nurses and drank tea. Sometimes I fetched things for patients, when the nurses were out of the ward or attending other people; perhaps a drink or an extra blanket, but normally I was beside Mary. I frequently checked her pulse, but it was very regular and only a little faster than normal. I constantly willed her to die. Would she never weaken? It was long past the three hours that she had been given to live.

The medicine bottles containing the drug, had been left in the ward with the night nurses. In one of them, were the capsules that David Jones had collected for the purpose of letting the hospital authorities know which drug Mary had taken, and in what quantity. I counted nineteen, so Mary had swallowed one hundred and eight-one, which amounted to well over four grams. I saw that a number of those nineteen were partly chewed, showing that she had been trying to get them down, until she could no longer do so. It was further proof of her courage and determination, and it accounted for her 'burnt' mouth. She had eaten, rather than swallowed them.

With dawn, the normal life of the hospital began to return. Patients were roused to wash, to be given medicines, and to eat breakfast. The screens were removed from Mary's bed to reveal us to the curious glances of the other people in the ward; a woman moaning and twitching incessantly, and a man beside her, who was holding her hand and crying silently.

I had spared two minutes the previous evening to telephone June. She told me later that my account of the events, since leaving her flat, had been muddled and confusing. She had been very worried, but forced by the circumstances to wait for long hours for me to telephone. I had not dared to contact anyone else. I needed support, but before the decision was made not to treat Mary, I feared that if I asked friends to come they would, like everyone else that evening, oppose me. Another factor, which even at that critical time influenced me, was my pride. I could not ask favours from those friends who had deserted Mary in the past years, or those who had stayed away from her in the last few weeks. When Mary was turned over to nursing care at midnight, it had seemed much too late, and also unnecessary, to telephone the only two friends who had remained consistently loyal to her.

The moment that I found someone to watch over Mary for a few minutes on that Monday morning, I left her bedside to telephone my friend, John. Briefly, I explained what had happened, and where he would find me. At 8.30, within one hour of my call, he came up to the hospital. Before entering the ward he had been instructed not to stay for longer than fifteen minutes. This was unaccountable by any rational and humane standards. It was known and accepted that Mary was dying. I told John to ignore the instruction and to remain longer.

Very little was said by either of us. It was unnecessary. The sight of Mary was enough. I pulled back the covers and indicated to him all her bruises and lacerations. John took her hand and bent over to talk to her. Although her open eyes were sightless, she recognised his voice and felt his hand round hers. She managed to utter just one word, "John".

I slipped away and went outside to my car. The dog had been shut inside for twelve hours. I had to walk him. Whilst I was in the hospital grounds I saw Dr Hickman, and hurried over to ask for his opinion on Mary's chance of survival. He answered that he was not certain, but he added that, if Mary did survive, he intended to see the resident psychiatrist with a view, as he termed it, to 'getting your wife into hospital, where she will receive proper medical care'.

Reacting instantly with rage, I raised my fist to strike him, but he quickly stepped back to avoid the blow. In the accident wing during the previous evening, I had frequently emphasized that Mary might eventually be committed to hospital, where she might deteriorate to the condition of the patient with H.C., whom she had nursed a few years earlier. Hickman might have seriously considered consulting with the resident psychiatrist, but his specific naming of St. Giles betrayed his malice towards me.

I was not only enraged by Hickman's words, but frightened that if Mary did survive, she might be committed to an institution under a section of the Mental Health Act. It was unbearable to contemplate her magnificent courage leading to such an end. Hurriedly, I bundled my dog back into the car and went to a telephone. My problems were multiplying; would I never emerge from the nightmare?

I telephoned my neighbour, Alan, and asked for his advice on this latest threat to Mary. He was uncertain and advised me to contact 'Mind, The National Association for Mental Health'. I did not want to make telephone calls from a public box requiring coins and with other difficulties that might be protracted and keep me away from Mary's side, so instead, I made a quick call to June. She telephoned 'Mind', and they sent her information on the Mental Health Act by return post. It was not reassuring when I read it the following morning.

The 1959 Act is too long and complex to be quoted here. Briefly, it confers very wide-ranging powers upon social workers, doctors, psychiatrists, and even the police, to commit people to mental institutions without reference to their nearest relative. Further, under Section 52, a County Court has the power to take away the rights of the nearest relative. Clearly, if Hickman and the resident psychiatrist decided to send Mary to St Giles, I would be powerless to stop them.

John left following my call to June, and I settled down again beside Mary. As the morning slowly passed she seemed to grow stronger, and her pulse slackened to a near normal rate. I was appalled when thinking of the possible consequences, should she survive. I never left her other than for occasional visits to the toilet, and my tears rarely stopped flowing.

The exhausting monotony of the vigil was broken mid-morning by the consultant and his cortege. I observed the solicitous care he showed for his patients as he moved from one to another, but Mary did not receive a glance when he walked past her bed, nor did he give me a supportive word. Although she was dying we were ignored, and her status as a non-patient was symbolised by the stark absence of a clip board that hung at the foot of all the other beds.

Later in the morning Morag and her daughter came, having been telephoned by my friend, John. Morag confided to me that she thought Mary should have done it long ago. Her daughter nodded her approval for my stand in not allowing Mary to be treated, and wept over her saying, "We all love you, Mary".

I took advantage of their presence to telephone Joan. I quickly explained what had happened, and asked her to sit with Mary that night. I had been without sleep for two nights with an exhausting day between, and I could not watch continually over her. Joan sounded frightened at the prospect of acting as a nurse, and begged to be excused from the duty. She also pleaded that she could not leave friends, who happened to be staying with her at that time on a brief visit from overseas.

These calls, to John and to Joan, were the only ones I made to friends that day. But the news of Mary's suicide attempt quickly spread from them to others. That afternoon and evening a few of them gathered at different times around her bed. Without exception, they agreed with my stand in not allowing Mary to be medicated. This concurrence was unprecedented, contrasting with the ambivalence that they had shown in the preceding years on the issues raised by H.C.. If they had given me unreserved moral support from the start of the illness, I would not have felt so frustrated and directed so much of my anger against Mary.

In spite of this unanimity, most of them gave me little or no practical help. I knew that the situation might continue for several days before its resolution, so it was necessary for me to make practical arrangements to cover them. I needed someone to take the dog, and John offered to keep him for a few days, but his wife would not agree to the arrangement. Only two months earlier their son had died suddenly, and admittedly, her grief was fresh and vivid, but I could not help remembering that Mary, who was in a desperate plight herself, seeking the means to bring about her own suicide, had held Anne's hand at the time to comfort her. None of the other friends offered to have the dog, nor did they suggest any alternative arrangement. It was John who on his own initiative telephoned local kennels until he found one that would take him, in spite of his geriatric state, provided I delivered the dog to them. The problem was solved by June, who arranged with her employer to take annual leave so that she could remain at home to keep the dog in her flat.

My most pressing need though, was for someone to sit with Mary so that I could sleep. I fared only marginally better in this respect. Claudia, who later was to provide a linkage cover early Tuesday morning, was otherwise too busy with political canvassing, and Morag, apart from watching Mary so that I could slip home for a meal, was too involved with her grandchildren. It was left to Jane to give me unstinting support.

It was Monday afternoon when she heard what had happened. She attempted to speak with me by telephone, but I refused. It is to her credit that she ignored this snub and made her way to the hospital. From that moment, with her energy and practical nursing skills, she took control of the situation.

In the afternoon I rushed home for a quick meal and a bath, and then drove on to collect my friend John from his home. As we were leaving to return to the hospital, I casually remarked how cruel life was, their son taken in his prime, and now Mary, who deserved to die peacefully, was lingering. To my surprise Anne exclaimed, with spirit, that "God takes in His time, not ours". Despite my exhausted state, this starkly critical reference to Mary's suicide shocked me because of its primitive, fundamentalist inhumanity. I said nothing, but John replied with great dignity, "Anne, you are speaking to two non-believers".

We returned to the hospital to find that Mary had been examined by the House Doctor, the first doctor to look at her since she had entered the ward. Through a nurse, I was told that Mary should be catheterized. I did not trust the hospital staff to make a distinction between nursing care, designed to relieve Mary's suffering, and positive treatment conducive towards her survival. With Jane's timely arrival, I was able to turn to her for advice before agreeing to the doctor's recommendation.

That night Jane sat with Mary and I was able to take a full night's sleep. By Jane's account, she, too, had been unable to leave Mary's side except for short periods, the delirium continuing unabated. Jane, like me, had to guard constantly against Mary falling out of bed, and to comfort her when her distress became most acute.

Following complaints from other patients that they were kept awake by Mary, she was moved on Tuesday morning to a private room. It was a considerable improvement to be no longer in public view. At times through her babbling, I would detect a plea from her for a cigarette, and although I dared not light one, I would hold an unlit one as a surrogate to her lips, and she would greedily draw on it. Sometimes, she would call on the dog by name, and then tell him to "Get down, get down", and go through the motion of pushing him away. Her restless movements caused her to slide down the bed, and repeatedly I would heave her up to get her head on to the pillows. She was sufficiently aware to be able to help me by pushing with her arms and legs.

John came in the afternoon and I was able to go into the hospital grounds for a short break. He did not sit beside Mary, preferring to stand leaning over her bed for the extra contact that it gave. Mary showed no sign of weakening, and John observing this, said on my return, that if she did survive she would need loving care from me. I did not answer him. No less than John I knew what Mary needed, but I also knew that I could not produce that love. If she lived I would, in a short time, have to flee from her. Once more I cursed the society that allowed the disease to flourish unchecked, and the individuals who had been directly responsible for Mary's birth. I remembered what Mary had so often said, "First they give you the disease, and then you're left to get on with it."

In the evening, Jane came with a collection of items to ease Mary's suffering.

Glycerine to swab her burnt mouth and lips, Eau de Cologne, a comb and brush, a flannel, and a drinking beaker. Her husband accompanied her and, on entering the room, made a remark in his inimitably pusillanimous manner about how sorry he was to see Mary in such a condition. He, as much as any friend, had consistently been evasive regarding the moral issues raised by the disease, and he had shown an uncharacteristic lack of intelligence towards understanding the basic facts of H.C.. He was not without interest in public affairs, expressing this interest by political canvassing during elections. His words angered me, and I snarled at him that if he were really sorry, he would do something about it and write a few letters, starting with one to his Member of Parliament.

I left Jane with Mary for two hours to go home for a bath and a meal. I returned to find that she had persuaded the hospital staff to provide rigid cot sides for the bed. She had also dressed Mary's wounds and laid out the various comforts professionally on the bedside table. Mary had lain in the hospital for forty eight hours. As I recall, she had been catheterized the previous day and sponged once by the nursing orderlies, but nothing more. When I saw what Jane had done, and the organisation that she had brought to easing Mary's suffering, I realised that when it was agreed not to give treatment, it was also tacit policy by the hospital to give minimum nursing care. Mary's signal act of courage was unrecognised, and she continued to suffer from injustice and indifference, even as she lay dying.

Jane took me aside to say that, whilst I should give Mary sips of water whenever she wanted it, I must not allow her to drink, because that might prolong her life. I pointed out to Jane that Mary had not eaten since Saturday, nor had she been at rest for a moment, so surely she must soon weaken. Jane disagreed, giving as an example hunger-strikers who live without food for as long as two months. Jane then gripped my arm and said, "If she does survive, be a man, set it up for her, and then go out, so that next time it works".

Jane left, promising to be back the following morning to care for Mary through Wednesday. It was arranged that I would relieve her early in the evening, but beyond that no plans had been made. I was apprehensive, believing that I might have to face the impossible task of managing Mary alone for the remainder of the week.

That Tuesday night Mary appeared to grow in strength, twisting and turning more vigorously than ever. I constantly hauled her up the bed, or on to her back when she rolled over, threatening to dislodge the catheter. If ever I left her side she was immediately aware that I had gone, and would attempt to climb over the cot sides to follow me. The dressings on her arms and legs frequently slipped out of position and had to be re-adjusted. She never stopped moaning and babbling, and her wide-open, sightless eyes continually rolled. As I stood and watched her violent chorea, in that cot-sided bed, it occurred to me that I was witnessing a grim parody at speed, of the final weeks or months of an H.C. victim in an institution.

At times throughout the night, nurses came in to talk to me, or to bring me tea, and I outlined her story to two or three of them. An Irish nurse hoped that I would be given the Grace to continue, but chiefly, I remember a cheerful West Indian nurse who helped me to re-dress Mary's wounds and to straighten the bedclothes, and who sat with her, so that I could go outside into the cool night air for a break.

It was a dreadful night, and I was in despair. I had slept only one night in four and I was exhausted. Jane's early morning arrival was so welcome that I hugged her, and with faltering voice told her how awful the night had been. I then left the hospital and drove to June. She gave me sleeping tablets and put me to bed.

* * *

I woke in the afternoon to June shaking me and saying that the hospital had telephoned. There had been a change in Mary's condition and they

192

wanted me there. She helped me to dress and led me out to the car. Although she had not driven for two or three years, there was no question of who would drive. Without a word, she took the keys from me and sat in the driving seat. I was too tired and drugged to have any clear thoughts on the reason why I was wanted urgently. I remember the journey only for the novelty of the double vision that June's sleeping tablets had induced in me.

At the hospital we were met by a nursing sister, who said that my wife had died. I could not believe it. Her words were too simple to describe adequately such a momentous event. Mary had been alive, very alive, a few hours earlier, and I was being told that she was dead. It was too great a change to have taken place in such a short space of time. It must be a mistake.

"Would you like to see her?" I was asked.

"Yes", I nodded, and we walked down the corridor to Mary's room.

She was tightly tucked in the bed with only her head showing. Her face was grey, her eyes closed, her mouth slightly open, and she was completely still. I bent over to touch her cheek, and unaccountably started to pull away the covers, but hands from behind took me by the shoulders and I was led away.

Jane and Joan were standing waiting in a small lounge off the corridor. They explained that Mary had become fully conscious, and the hospital staff had wanted to overrule me in my absence and treat her. Anxiously they had asked her if she wanted this. At first she had answered, "Yes", but with full realisation of her situation she had changed it to "No", and gone into a spasm of angry frustration. She had turned blue, her heart having stopped, and died.

Their description of her end reminded me of her anger whenever I had suggested that she did not really wish to die. Her heart failure could possibly be accounted for by the action of the drug, which was reputed to depress its function.

* * *

I woke the following morning and remembered everything with great relief. My ordeal was over. The burden of responsibility, which I had carried, had gone. I was numb and weary, but I felt free. There would be an inquest, and later that day, June drove me to the hospital where we met the Coroner's clerk, who noted down a few administrative details that I gave to him. Following this routine work, he said that there were young children at risk to Huntington's chorea in the area, and they did not wish it to be revealed at the inquest that my wife had suffered from the disease. I refused, amazed that the Coroner's policy was to promote the conspiracy of silence surrounding H.C.. The clerk then mused that the disease was like second-generation suicide. No, I raged inwardly, it is N th generation suicide, whilst affected families continue to have children.

But the interview was not over. It ended with a casual, but alarming remark from him that he would have to give a copy of his report to the Director of Public Prosecutions.

I broke off from all the routine business that follows any death, and went up to the Release office. It had been my intention to give them a full description of Mary's suicide at a later date, but this statement by the clerk precipitated it. Mary was a marked woman on files held by the C.I.D., and they might be looking for a direct connection between her suicide and her possession of the Guide. Release must be alerted because there was a possibility that they might be prosecuted for aiding or abetting suicide, under Section II of the Suicide Act.

The Release staff were appreciative of my warning visit and confirmed what I suspected, that it is not normal for Coroner's reports of suicides to be referred to the Director of Public Prosecutions. They then recorded all the details of Mary's suicide.

Later that year, the Attorney General applied to the High Court for A Declaration that it is an offence against Section II of the Suicide Act, for the Euthanasia Society to distribute the Guide. The case was heard and judgement given in April, 1983.

The judge would not grant a Declaration, because he did not wish to usurp the jurisdiction of the criminal courts. This ruling was more than ambiguous, it was a refusal to make a decision. At the time of writing the position is unchanged, and it is not clear if distribution of the Guide is an offence.

Let this story of Mary's search for the means to deliver herself from the horrors of Huntington's chorea be a testimony to the moral improbity of the Attorney General's attempt to suppress the Guide. Let her suffering be evidence of the moral turpitude of successive Governments who permitted her birth, continue to permit the transmission of the disease, and refuse to change the Law, in order to allow the victims of the disease to escape from its ravages.

* * *

John helped me to clean the bedroom, where I had found Mary. We discovered that she had inserted large plastic bags beneath the bottom sheet of the bed. As a nurse, she would be conscious that her bowels might move at the moment of death, and she did not wish to ruin the mattress and give additional trouble to me. This calculated act was further proof of her calm and stoical courage.

We also found that she had laid in an excessive amount of food on her last shopping outing with Joan, who at the time noted it, but did not understand its significance. To the end, Mary had shown her loving concern for me by ensuring that I would have an ample supply of food in the house, following her death.

Latterly, Mary had become a compulsive smoker, but there were no cigarette stubs in the ashtrays, nor any in the waste bin. This was reasonable proof that she had made the attempt soon after I had left her at 1.30 p.m. on Saturday. She had lain alone for thirty hours, before I returned.

* * *

The morning of the funeral was dark and cloudy. John and I were the only mourners. A notice board outside the chapel listed the day's cremations. Only hers said, 'No minister'. June had made a spray of daffodils and cypress branches taken from my garden. Mary would have seen them thirteen days earlier. I placed it on the waiting coffin, the only splash of colour in that sombre setting.

We followed the coffin into the chapel and it was placed upon the bier. Then we were alone, and whilst I stood a few yards away John placed his hand upon it and, in a strong clear voice breaking into the silence, spoke a farewell message.

"Dear Mary, we don't know why you had to go. We will all miss you very much; we are desolate now that you have gone. We all remember your courage; we are not so brave as you...............................Goodbye, dear Mary".

He turned and silently left the chapel. I stood alone beside the bier for a moment, silent, weeping silently, before following him out.

* * *

Ten days later there remained one more duty for me to discharge. John and I drove out to the Chilterns, and walked down the hillside below Ibstone, to the spot where Mary and I had sat overlooking the Turville Valley, on that last Friday of her life. We cleared a little ground beside the hedge and planted forget-me-nots and daffodils. Then I scattered her ashes. She was no more tangible than her dust that would soon merge with the earth and, with the termination of our memories when we followed her into oblivion, she would be expunged for ever.

* * *

In spite of the request made to me by the Coroner's clerk not to reveal that Mary had suffered from Huntington's chorea, at the inquest the Coroner encouraged me to speak freely about Mary, and myself, and the disease. He made no attempt at any time to silence me, and his verdict was, 'She took her own life as a consequence of her knowledge that she was suffering from Huntington's chorea.'

* * *

At the time of writing, attention is focused upon the possibility of predictive tests for people at risk of H.C.. Research workers hope to achieve this in the near future, but I fail to see how tests can lead to the eradication of the disease, rather, their use would produce fresh problems. It is unlikely that people would be prepared to undergo a test, with the certainty that many would learn that they have the mutant gene and therefore must fall victim to the disease. There would also be the additional problem, with consequential stress upon affected family relationships, which would arise if a young person submits to a test that, if positive, would also condemn their at-risk parent.

Addendum

Since this story was written, Huntington's chorea has been renamed Huntington's Disease, voluntary euthanasia is now called assisted dying and Release has been replaced by 'Dignity in Dying'. Opinion polls show that more than 80% of people are in favour of assisted dying, but this has not been democratically reflected by a change to the 1961 Suicide Act.

In 2009 Debbie Purdy, who suffered with Multiple Sclerosis, secured a Law Lords' ruling which asked for clarification on prosecution policy for cases of assisted dying from Keir Starmer, the then Director of Public Prosecutions. In response, he was forced to publish guidelines on his previously unknown policy. It listed many reasons for and against prosecution but, significantly, one stated that professional medical people would more likely be charged and lay people less likely. My wife's shocking D.I.Y. suicide was, and remains, a strong pointer to the perversity of this part of the policy which is a deterrent to effective medical assistance. It reinforces the need for primary parliamentary legislation to remove the morass of uncertainty surrounding assisted dying.

My own involvement in the debate came when I was asked by Dignity in Dying, early in 2010, to go on TV. I made several appearances, but it was a Newsnight programme, when I divulged that I had given assistance to my wife's suicide, that led to notable consequences.

A team from the BBC came out to film and question me. They were at my house for four and three quarter hours but, when screened, their material had been edited down to a few minutes and presented as if my wife's suicide had been motivated by her distress at the sight of mine. My doubts when agreeing to go on an edited programme, were amply justified.

This distortion by Newsnight was uncritically accepted in part of an editorial article in 'The Independent'. I wrote to the paper giving a factual account for publication, but it wasn't even acknowledged!

Regional TV and the local press were immediately on to my story, and whilst the publicity was uncomfortable, it was scrupulously fair and accurate in its reporting.

Soon after, the inevitable 'phone call came from the police; a London C.I.D. Officer wanted to interview me. We met at a local police station where I was immediately arrested, bureaucratically processed, photographed, hand and finger printed, DNA profiled and a lengthy statement by me recorded on tapes. Finally, after three hours, I was bailed to reappear at a later date. The arresting officer and local police adhered carefully to their guidelines explaining my rights and, at all times, were polite and considerate.

Twice I answered bail, but each time the C.I.D. failed to arrive. The second time the local police handed me the 'phone inviting me to speak to them. They said that in future they would contact me. This uncertainty led me to make a formal complaint to the Independent Police Complaints Commission, asking to be either released from bail or charged. This was acknowledged, but I was to be held on bail for more than one year.

I was not unduly perturbed, but Keir Starmer later revealed that other people, in similar situations to mine, were on bail whilst he deliberated on their cases. They could well have been suffering extreme worry fresh from harrowing experiences like mine.

There was a postscript. Following my release from bail, two middle rank police officers came out from London to ensure that I was satisfied with the result, and paid my travel expenses.

There have been attempts over the years to change the law and as recently as 2015, a very weak and limited private members' bill on assisted dying was debated in the Commons. Counter to their constituents' beliefs, it was decisively defeated. This contrasted with the alacrity with which Brexit was triggered following the 2016 Referendum result, with its slender majority, of those who voted, of 52% to 48%.

Stephen Sedley, who was an appeal court judge, asked in an article on assisted dying in the London Review Of Books in 2015, 'Why are MPs so out of kilter with public opinion? Part of the answer may be fear for their seats. Any votes to be won by support for assisted dying are eclipsed by the damage that can be done.....' The obvious rider to his observation, is that the primary motive of most MPs is to further their ambitions.